WHY DO CATHOLICS GENUFLECT?

Why Do Catholics Genuflect?

And Answers to Other Puzzling Questions
About the Catholic Church

AL KRESTA

CHARIS

SERVANT PUBLICATIONS
ANN ARBOR, MICHIGAN

Charis Books is an imprint of Servant Publications especially designed to serve Roman Catholics.

NIHIL OBSTAT: Rev. Msgr. Sylvester L. Fedewa, S.T.L., D.Min.
                 Censor Librorum
IMPRIMATUR: Most Reverend Carl F. Mengeling
                 Bishop of Lansing
                 September 6, 2001

The NIHIL OBSTAT and IMPRIMATUR are a declaration that a book or pamphlet is considered to be free from doctrinal or moral error. It is not implied that those who have granted the NIHIL OBSTAT and IMPRIMATUR agree with the contents, opinions or statements expressed.

Servant Publications
P.O. Box 8617
Ann Arbor, MI 48107

Cover design by Brian Fowler, DesignTeam, Grand Rapids, Michigan

03 04 10 9 8 7 6 5

Printed in the United States of America
ISBN 1-56955-243-6

LIBRARY OF CONGRESS CATALOGING-IN-PUBLICATION DATA

Kresta, Al.
    Why do Catholics genuflect? : and answers to other puzzling questions about the Catholic Church / Al Kresta.
        p. cm.
    Includes bibliographical references.
    ISBN 1-56955-243-6 (alk. paper)
    1. Catholic Church–Doctrines—Miscellanea. I. Title.
    BX1754.3 .K74 2001
    282—dc21

                                                    2001005339

Contents

Acknowledgements and Dedications

This book has taken shape in the midst of the most hectic circumstances but under the most patient auspices. When Bert Ghezzi first approached me about doing a book for Servant, I seriously overestimated my discretionary time. As my staff and I were shopping billboard locations to promote our radio network, I kept hoping to find one that would say, "Stop. Take six-month sabbatical to write book ... God." I never saw it.

This book was formed as I was responsible for launching the Ave Maria Radio Network; opening, outfitting, and staffing two radio stations; and syndicating my talk show, *Kresta in the Afternoon*. My entire staff has paid a price for my failure to estimate my time properly. I am grateful for their indulgence.

On the family front, we've been tossed to and fro between life and death. My youngest sister passed away, my oldest child went off to college, and my wife brought forth her fifth child with the help of the Lord. Through all this, Bert Ghezzi and Paul Thigpen at Servant Books have shown great reservoirs of grace and intelligence. Nevertheless, if the book has any screwy ideas in it, blame Paul and Bert; they should have caught them.

I'd like to dedicate this book to four non-Catholic couples with whom I've co-labored over the years in the field of Christian ministry. Each, in his or her own way, knows the cost of discipleship, and for that they have won my admiration. When our family entered the Catholic Church, the most resistance I received from any of them was respectful perplexity.

To Len and Clara Simons: No friend is truer than the one who will tell you the truth and still carry you when you've been wounded.

Clara, without the gift of that trip to the Holy Land with Sally, the Krestas may not have ended up at Christ the King Catholic Church.

To Paul and Beth Patton: Your affirmation and encouragement, your opening of doors to ministry, ended up charting my life. Kind of scary, isn't it?

To Bob and Evelyn Hoey: Our ministerial tracks ran parallel for so long that I can't help but think that somehow, somewhere, in the providence of God, there will be a convergence again.

To Roger and Linda Stieg: You will always remain dear to me as the first couple God allowed me to help to an adult understanding of Jesus' work. Seeing you again recently reminded me of how important it is to seek the Truth always. You have and, I'm convinced, you always will.

I'd also like to dedicate this book to Linda Denniston, who, not knowing I had returned to the Catholic Church, innocently asked me to talk to a boyfriend about why he should leave the Church. Linda, you had no idea what you were getting into, did you?

From that request, hundreds of people have attended my "Bridge Groups." (No, it's not about cards.) In these groups twenty to thirty Catholics and non-Catholics come together—already accepting one another as fellow Christians—to discuss, with varying degrees of passion and intelligence, the things that divide us the most: papacy, purgatory, Mary, saints, and the Eucharist.

To all my listeners throughout my nearly fifteen years of broadcasting both as an evangelical Protestant and as an evangelical Catholic: for their support, good humor, and great questions. You made this book.

As anybody who loves books will quickly discern, I'm indebted to innumerable authors, speakers, bards, polemicists, expositors, and wise guys. They have given me far more than I can footnote, and since I have a hand-me-down mind, I pass it along to you. My goal hasn't been originality but fidelity.

Introduction

Why *do* Catholics genuflect?

Catholics genuflect because we are in rehearsal for that regenerating moment at the end of history "when every knee shall bow and every tongue confess that Jesus is Lord to the glory of God the Father" (Phil 2:10-11). We're a little slow at learning, and so we thought we'd begin early.

Genuflection is such a small thing. We bend the right knee to the floor and rise up again before a holy person or object. But it's a little gesture that demonstrates some big things: repentance, petition, veneration.

It means that Catholics believe that there is something beyond this material world that we turn to, appeal to, and honor. It means we aren't a law unto ourselves. It means we believe that there is a principle of hierarchy in the universe to which we submit.

In this simple act lies a whole view of God, man, time, eternity, sin, salvation, spirit, and matter. It is a small but submissive response to what God has done in revealing himself to us.

Revelation

God not only exists; he communicates with us. We are not thrown back on the mere resources of our own personal experience or speculation. But while Christianity is profoundly revelational, it is also the greatest champion of reason. The laws of logic are anchored in the Logos—that is, the "Word" himself (see Jn 1:1).

Right reasoning is not just patterned neural responses in the brain. It actually conforms to the external world. Reality is not just a biochemical show between our ears. Right reasoning can discover that reality.

Consequently, we are to love the Lord our God with all our *mind* (see Mt 22:37). Faith is not mere sentiment. As the celebrated Catholic writer Flannery O'Connor has observed: "Sentimentality is to Christianity what pornography is to love." Faith engages the entire person.

The Catholic Church teaches that human reason can deduce the existence of God. Reason, however, is not adequate to discern certain of his attributes. So God has revealed himself to us in Scripture, in Christ, and in the teaching of his apostles, thereby supplementing what we can know through our reason and experience alone.

Human beings are blessed with a vantage point from beyond the flux of space and time. We've heard a Voice from beyond our own condition. Faith may have to move in the dark from time to time, but it isn't blind. As the noted evangelical writer Francis Schaeffer put it in one of his book titles: *He Is There and He Is Not Silent.*

Imagine yourself climbing a mountain in the Rockies. The fog has set in. You are uncertain what lies beyond the fog. You feel your way along the ledge step by step.

Suddenly a voice from across a valley startles you. "Stop! You are nearing a precipice. Back up ten feet and leap off the ledge, and you will find a firm landing fifteen feet below. You'll be safe."

You don't act immediately but shout back, "How do you know this?" He replies that he is a veteran climber of these parts and is perched on a cliff slightly above you and can see clearly.

You must trust him. You must have faith in him. But it is a reasonable, not a blind, faith.

In our own day there is a new appreciation for divine revelation. We have passed through the crucible of modernity and emerged realizing that the skeptical project of the Enlightenment has failed. It could not meet the fundamental human need for something transcendent.

As creatures made in the image and likeness of God, we are hardwired for communion with him. "Our hearts are restless," St. Augustine prayed, "until they find their rest in Thee." Therefore our most basic aspirations and cravings for love, significance, meaning, purpose, and justice demand fulfillment.

Deep within, we know that we are not the measure of all things, nor is this world the end of all things. We actually do live in a universe where spiritually hungry men can find bread.

But the West has passed through a long and heady period of experimentation in rejecting the divine. In the eighteenth century our cultural elites began dismissing the intellectual trustworthiness of the Bible. In the nineteenth century some proclaimed the "death of God" idea as a culturally powerful force.

Finally, the twentieth century shocked us into realizing that if God is dead, so too is man. The radical experiments of atheistic communism and neo-pagan National Socialism pursued a policy based on the assumption that man has no ultimate meaning and can be used by commissars, party leaders, and the Reich as cannon fodder, without any fear of or appeal to a Higher Court.

Now as we enter the twenty-first century, revelational claims proliferate. For many people, the question isn't "Has God spoken?" but "Which god has spoken?" Our problem today is not necessarily skepticism about the possibility of divine revelation, but rather a cheapening of all revelational claims, since there are so many.

For many historical, rational, and existential reasons which are beyond the scope of this book, I came to believe that the eternal God has disclosed himself most clearly and accurately through the Hebrews of ancient Israel and through Jesus of Nazareth, who rose from the dead. At the risk of sounding flippant, if I have to choose between competing revelational claims, I'm going to believe the guy who plausibly presents himself as victor over death to many eyewitnesses (see Lk 1:1-3; Jn 19:35; Acts 1:1-8, 1 Cor 15:3-8; 2 Pt 1:16; 1 Jn 1:1-4, and other scriptural passages).

I just can't get away from trusting the evidence of my senses and consequently the sense reports of fellow creatures who strike me as trustworthy. For a wide variety of reasons, the New Testament writers have enlisted my trust and confidence. They are good witnesses.

There is another modern objection to divine revelation based more on political and civil concerns than rational. The charge is that claims to possess the truth render a person intolerant. Many like to distinguish between "truth possessed" and "truth pursued."

"Truth pursued," allegedly, makes you a good citizen. "Truth possessed" makes you prejudiced, bigoted, and dogmatic. This is crudely put, but the truth is that those who would make such a charge themselves believe they possess some primitive or rudimentary notion of the truth, which they are pursuing. Otherwise, how would they expect to recognize the truth when they come across it?

The real question is this: Do we claim *exhaustive* knowledge or merely *accurate* knowledge? We can possess truth without possessing it exhaustively.

In all cultures and at all times—certainly in the midst of today's global transformations—people ask the same basic questions about the meaning of life: Who am I? Where have I come from and where am I going? Why is there evil? What is there after this life?

So what is the value of asking such questions if they can't be answered? After all, who quests for what he thinks he won't find? It leads to always walking toward the horizon and never arriving home. The distinction between the truth possessed and the truth pursued is a distinction without a difference.

Let's make it simple: If we claim to have The Truth exhaustively, we are claiming to be God, and that is dangerous. Only at the end of time will we know God as he has known us, and we will see him face-to-face (see 1 Cor 13:12).

Some Christians, however, have been so intimidated by the charge that the Truth is not accessible that they have tried to make a virtue of their ignorance and disbelief. At a recent Catholic education conference, for example, the keynote speaker said: "So what shall we teach about reality? What vision shall we give? What questions shall we ask? What map shall we ourselves use this time to chart the unknown? One drawn from past realities, or one hard gotten by walking new and unknown territory ourselves? Welcome to ambiguity!"

This is more like a cheer for the emperor's new clothes than a genuine invitation to the gospel. While the gospel is a mystery, it is not ambiguity. We seek clarity as well as charity. Tragically, for many the only absolute truth is that there are no absolute truths, and so they are doomed to live in a muddle, a fog, everybody with his or her own "reality."

Further, while the Catholic faith is rooted in antiquity, it is not antique. For the speaker quoted above, apparently, whatever is old is passé. I remember a line I learned in my early twenties that he who marries the spirit of the age soon becomes a widower. That speaker fears she will be out of step with her generation and thus miss the opportunity to live fully now within the customs of her own age.

One Eastern Orthodox writer put it this way: "Jesus did not say, 'I am the custom,' but 'I am the life.'" Yes, the Catholic faith has a past, but it is in the future that the Faith will be fully realized. Our past has launched our future.

As much as we respect reason and personal experience, divine revelation is central to Catholic faith. Christ Jesus is a mystery, but he is no muddle.

Christ

Why do Catholics genuflect?

Catholics genuflect because we are often in the presence of the Supreme Revelation, who is not a piece of data but a glorious Person. "Jesus Christ is the redeemer of the human race and is the center of human history and the cosmos," as Pope John Paul II says in beginning his first encyclical. Socrates asked, What is truth? Buddha taught the Four Noble Truths. Mohammed claimed to bear witness to the truth. But only Jesus of Nazareth dared to say, "I am ... the truth" (Jn 14:6).

For the Christian, Jesus is not the founder of a new religion but the revealer of ultimate reality. This ultimate reality, however, is not something disconnected from our experience in the world. "The acceptance of life as it is must teach us trust and humility. This is because every *real* experience of life is an experience of God."[1]

Jesus is the light and the lens by which we see the world with all its astonishing detail and diversity. You might call this the "epistemological" significance of Christ: he reveals God to us, and in the light of God we are able to make sense of our own mysterious selves and the external world of creation.

Christ is not only the atoning sacrifice for our sins and the answer for problems of conscience, guilt, and morality, but he is also the resolution of metaphysical disputes about time and eternity, faith and reason, body and soul, matter and spirit, spirituality and sexuality. He restores us to a unitary vision of life, where all these false polarizations are reconciled. That is why we genuflect. He is the great Teacher. We are the teachable students. We kneel before him.

Sacrament

Catholics are probably most commonly seen genuflecting in front of the Blessed Sacrament—the Eucharist reserved in the tabernacle, displayed in a prominent place within a local parish church. Here we are the knights kneeling before our King. The Eucharist is the Body, Blood, Soul, and Divinity of Jesus. It makes visible under the appearance of bread and wine his broken body and shed blood.

Christ's saving death on Calvary is removed from us by nearly two thousand years of history. But it becomes contemporaneous with us through the Sacrament. We might say that the Eucharist is an extension of the Incarnation. Christ's Body continues as a material presence in the world.

The most simple definition of a sacrament is "an efficacious sign of grace, instituted by Christ and entrusted to the Church, by which divine life is dispensed to us through the work of the Holy Spirit." In other words, God is about showing as much as telling, image as much as word.

When the great Russian dancer Pavlova was asked what a certain dance meant, she answered, "If I could have spoken it, I wouldn't have danced it." If words were enough, God wouldn't have localized his Son in the Person of an itinerant Jewish preacher. But God loves space and time, and he wanted to dance within it.

The sacraments are the acts or if you wish, the "dances" of Christ, and thus the Catholic faith is shamelessly sacramental. That is, it makes invisible realities visible so that human beings may come to know the invisible God and be united with him forever in eternity.

The physical world that God created—things that are evident to our senses—convey something real beyond themselves. An object may appear to be primarily one thing—water, bread, oil—but in reality it may be a carrier of spiritual life, a vehicle of some invisible mystery. For instance, marriage may appear to be a social convention to perpetuate the species. In Catholic thought, however, it is a sacrament making visible the relationship between Christ and his Church.

It is common in our world to separate the spiritual from the physical, the existential from the historical, fact from value, knowledge from act. A Catholic view of the world, however, joins together what modernity has rent asunder. For a Catholic, the spiritual interpenetrates the physical. One could even say that the physical is emblematic of the spiritual.

The material universe is ordered to a final end. It is not merely a brute fact. Value rides piggyback on facts, and the existentially significant is discovered in space and time—that is, in history. This is why faith cannot be reduced to an act of the mind or heart.

True religion may begin in the heart, but it can't end there. We are not pure spirits. As enfleshed creatures embedded in history, we must act out that inner conviction in quite material ways. Angels may not require this kind of action, but humans do.

This understanding of the world is grounded in the Christian belief in divine creation. The physical world is a good gift of God and intended as the medium by which he reveals himself to us. We cannot understand the Catholic faith without grasping how "good" is its materiality.[2]

We believe not only that God created the world, but that he entered it. Creation and Incarnation go hand in hand. When God sent his Son, heaven touched earth. This is the key doctrine for Catholics.

Heaven still embraces earth in a material way. We are not in a poorer condition than when Jesus or the apostles walked the earth. We are two thousand years into the new creation. The human race has begun anew.

Re-creation or regeneration is Creation regained. God's purpose in redemption is essentially the same as it was in creation. When we talk about human beings getting "saved" or "redeemed," this means that they have become what they were created to be. Redemption in Christ is nothing other than true "humanization," the reestablishing of man in his original dignity with dominion over the cosmos and co-regency with God.

Our understanding of sacrament, authority, and salvation all flow from this singular act in which the eternal God takes on human nature and sanctifies the earth and history, making the world a material vehicle for his loving will. This is why sacraments, sacramentals, art, imagery, gesture, incense, and priesthood are so important to Catholics. Catholics like the material world. Matter is a great idea. After all, it was *God's* idea.

Not all Christians quite get this point. Think of the hymn lyric: "The things of this world grow strangely dim in the light of his glory and grace." If by "the world" we mean sin, selfishness, the works of the flesh, then, of course, that's true. As we grow in grace we become less controlled by sin and idols.

But if we mean by these words that, as my love of God and longing for the kingdom grow, I don't notice sunsets and art and the needs of the poor, then it is an absolute lie. As evangelical spiritual writer Jerram Barrs has put it: "The truth is that if I'm truly in the 'light of God's glory and grace,' the world will never have seemed more bright to me. Everything becomes new, dear, wonderful. It is God's creation."

I suppose that before the Fall, Eden had no distinctively sacred places, no distinctively sacred rites, since all was sacred and unstained by sin. There was no need to elaborate a sacramental view of things because God was so present that he walked and talked with Adam and Eve in the cool of the day (see Gn 3:8).

At the time of the Fall, however, the true meaning of creation was obscured from us. It was as if a film covered over our eyes, dimming our perception of the real nature of things. We lost our vision of God and subsequently of man, his image. Immediately after the Fall, Adam blamed Eve, who had previously been cherished as the gift of God. You might also say we lost the true meaning of water, bread, oil, marriage, birth, death, and even suffering at the time of the Fall.

In redemption, however, Jesus—as the Sacrament of God—lifts that film and restores our vision. The Church, as the sacrament of Jesus, restores that vision and, in the seven sacraments, makes available again the true meaning of creation. The universe is no longer divided between matter and spirit, temporal and eternal, visible and invisible. Creation is restored to us as God intended it.

A sacramental view of life turns the dinner table into a rehearsal of the marriage supper of the Lamb, the workplace into a temple of dominion, the marriage bed into an altar for renewing the oath of our wedding covenant, sickness into a winepress of suffering that squeezes us into conformity with Christ. We light a candle and spread incense to make visible and tangible our prayers ascending to heaven. We dip our fingers in holy water and make the sign of the cross to recall us to our baptismal vows in the name of the Father, the Son, and the Holy Spirit.

We genuflect because we are in the presence of Glory. Perhaps at the close of history there will be no such need. All things will be restored, God will be all in all, and the entire cosmos will be his Temple (see 1 Cor 15:28; Rv 21:22-23). But for now, God rides astride the things he created.

One Church

When Jesus was asked, "Show us the Father," he said, "He who has seen me has seen the Father" (Jn 14:9). We claim that Jesus is the Sacrament of the Father. He makes him visible. The Church likewise is the Sacrament of Jesus and is being asked, "Show us Jesus." Our answer must be: "He who has seen Christ's body, the Church, has seen Jesus" (see Jn 17:20-26).

By taking on human flesh and occupying space and time, Christ gave us the central organizing principle of the community that today is his body on the earth. We might call this the "sociological" significance of the Incarnation. Christ willed as a key element of his Church that it be a visible, tangible society united to him both spiritually and historically. This body of Christ subsists within the Catholic Church and is the medium by which he operates in space and time, not only proclaiming redemption but also transmitting his very life.

When Christ Jesus calls a person to himself, he calls him to his body. This is not merely an invisible communion, but a visible one. Jesus the Christ is a living Person in the world today. He is the Head not only of the Church in heaven, but of the body on earth.

Together, Head and body constitute the whole Christ. Because of sin among the body's members, the body may not always get the signals from the Head very well and may even seem a little spastic. But it is Christ's mystical body, not mine. I cannot divide from it to go off and start my own church any more than someone in ancient Israel could complain about corrupt priests and kings and try to establish a thirteenth tribe of Israel. Catholics are committed to the visible, structured unity of God's people.

Catholics genuflect because Christ indwells the community he established. Catholics are able to recognize Christ even in the faces of all the poor and indigent, outcast and oppressed (see Mt 25:31-46). Jesus told the world that they could judge whether the Father sent the Son by the degree of observable love and unity that could be witnessed in his disciples (see Jn 17:21-23). This oneness must be observable not merely as a unity of Spirit but as a unity of structure with historically as well as spiritually defined leadership.

Christians must be one not only "spiritually," but also in a tangible, unified body—that is, what we might call "incarnationally." It is not enough to acquiesce in the belief that all true believers in Christ are invisibly joined together in the Spirit. This is of course true, but the divisions among Christians are a great scandal to the watching world. No attempt to spin doctrinal and institutional divisions as somehow a glorious diversity will persuade a critical observer who wants to know whether the Father sent the Son to be the Savior of the world.

The Catholic Church understands itself to be the steward of the visible unity of Christ's body. When all the doctrinal arguing is over, when all the punches and counterpunches are exhausted, the Catholic Church will still be standing—sometimes shouting, sometimes whimpering, that Christ willed visible unity for his people—and will still be working for a regathering of Christians for a common witness. This is essential to Catholic faith.[3]

Why do Catholics genuflect? Because we are in painful petition before God that Christ's body be once again restored as visibly one. So join us and "enter, let us bow down in worship; let us kneel before the Lord who made us. For this is our God, whose people we are, God's well-tended flock" (Ps 95: 6-7, NAB).

About This Book

This book is about answering questions, something I've done day in and day out for years as a teacher, pastor, editor, talk show host, and personal evangelist. Space limitations forbade my answering great questions about Catholic social teaching, the rosary, the stations of the cross, the liturgical year, the Church fathers, the possibility of women priests, and much more.

Rest assured it wasn't lack of interest, just space. So do us both a favor and buy lots of copies of this book, give them away, and then demand a second volume from the publisher. I've already got another fifty thousand words sitting in the can. I love questions and answers!

This book assumes that Christians—Catholics and non-Catholics— are family: a dysfunctional family, for certain, but definitely family. So I focus on what most divides us in order to move us to a greater unity. We've had a generation of building goodwill, and I think we can start, in a spirit of patience and charity, to clarify what keeps us apart.

After all, few people ask questions about the things upon which we are agreed. They want to know why we differ. So this book evidences a disproportionate interest in things Marian, papal, and sacramental, since these are the areas that most divide us.

With the exception of a few endnotes, I've tried to avoid scholarly apparatus. This book was not meant to be a definitive work of apologetics but rather a conversation that would help interested Catholics and non-Catholics better understand why Catholics believe and behave as we do.

I. Catholics' Relationship To Other Believers

Are Catholics Christians?

"Are Catholics Christians?" For many this may seem an odd question. Yet some people just beginning to seek God and pose spiritual questions are simply ignorant about the terms. They've heard that there are Christians of all stripes and want to know if Catholics are to be included in that vast body. It's an innocent question, much like asking, "Are Swedes Europeans?"

Others who ask the question, however, may carry about eccentric notions of Jesus that don't conform to the New Testament images of Christ. They conceive of him as meekly and mildly walking the shores of Galilee with dreamy eyes and a slightly pained expression on his face, as though he had an annoying pebble in his right sandal. When they hear that the Catholic Church accepts war under certain conditions, or doesn't champion vegetarianism, or restricts the sacrament of matrimony to heterosexuals intending a lifelong union with the intention of raising children, or denies that all dogs go to heaven, they say, "That's mean. Are Catholics really Christians?" They adhere to the "gospel of nice," which upon inquiry turns out to be little more than sentimental presumption.

A relatively small but especially vocal number of fellow Christians ask the question out of a doctrinal concern. They believe that the Catholic Church has distorted the gospel or added to it, and since the gospel is central to Christianity, they think the Catholic Church can't be Christian. I should add that they often have the same opinion of the Eastern Orthodox Church and deep suspicions about Anglicanism, Lutheranism, Presbyterianism, Methodism, and most historic Christian traditions.

Some Christians spend a lot of time trying to judge whether or not other professed Christians really believe the central teachings of

Christianity. This is an exercise in futility and may even be a sign of pride. In truth, none of us has the right to judge the interior state of another professed Christian.

A person's heart is transparent to God alone and, if the person has the grace of self-knowledge, maybe to himself as well. Those of us on the outside of the person can only know the content of his heart by his confession and his behavior. This is why Catholics rely on the observable sign of baptism and a willingness to profess the Creed as sufficient to welcome a fellow Christian into the family of God.

He may or may not believe these things deeply. He may or may not be very far along the road to union with God. But we include him in hope that God through the Church will grow him in the grace and knowledge of our Lord and Savior Jesus Christ.

So are Catholics Christians? Yes, all Catholics are Christians, but some are Christian in name only. This isn't much of an admission.

Are Baptists Christians? Are Episcopalians Christians? Are Presbyterians Christians? Like Catholics, all are Christians, but some in name only.

Even so, it's not a question Catholics tend to ask about others who are baptized, profess faith in Christ, and are part of a worshipping community. We accept them at face value as brothers and sisters in Christ, and most non-Catholics accept Catholics as fellow Christians. As noted above, though, some people have their doubts.

While there are some genuine doctrinal differences, much of the problem is manufactured by different vocabularies. Author Thomas Howard tells a story that cuts right through the tangle of words.

When I was received into the Catholic Church, I came to know an old woman named Sarah who came to daily Mass. At that same time, my octogenarian mother was living at our house. My mother, being a Protestant Evangelical who spent many hours with her Bible open in her lap, might have wondered about the sense in which it could be urged that Sarah was saved, not that my mother would have doubted Sarah's humility and sincerity (the two women have never met: I am only fancying the following vignette). But Sarah would have done poorly with a certain set of questions my mother might have put to her. "Are you saved?" Blank. "Well—are you born again?" Confusion. "Right. Have you accepted the Lord Jesus Christ as your personal Savior?" Consternation.

Just as my mother is concluding that her long-held fears about Catholics seem indeed to be well grounded, I interfere. I lead the two ladies over to a crucifix on the wall, and in my mother's hearing, I ask Sarah who that is. "Jesus." "Who is he?" "The Son of God." "What is he doing?" "Suffering death." "Why?" "For our sins."

And suddenly my mother has heard Sarah make a confession that qualifies Sarah for the category "saved." Sarah has believed all of this all along, and her trust is in this gospel, just as is my mother's. But left to themselves, the two ladies might have gone off deeply perplexed about each other's Christian credentials.[1]

All Christians share a common narrative about God, man, and the world. The Christian saga of salvation has four chapters. God created, man fell, Jesus redeemed and will come again to judge the living and the dead.

Catholics believe that the Triune God created the universe out of nothing. He created man, male and female, in his own image. After man's original disobedience ruptured the union between himself and God, introducing sin into the world, God began to work salvation on the earth through a series of covenants with Noah, Abraham, Moses, and David. Then he spoke through the prophets about a New Covenant by which he would restore mankind to union with himself. This New Covenant was inaugurated in the life and ministry of Jesus.

Jesus is the Second Person of the Trinity, a divine Person who took on human nature in the womb of the Virgin Mary and entered the world to redeem it. He demonstrated the kingdom of God through his miracles; gathered twelve apostles; was crucified under Pontius Pilate as an atonement for our sins; rose bodily from the dead; and commissioned the apostles to perpetuate his message through preaching the good news of the salvation wrought by Christ, teaching his commandments, baptizing, and celebrating the Lord's Supper.

Jesus then ascended to heaven, where he is seated at the right hand of the Father. The Holy Spirit was sent to constitute the Church, and Christ continues to govern his Church today. He will come again to judge the living and the dead. All those who believe these things should imitate Christ by living a life of holiness, loving sacrifice and service, and worship of God, always bearing witness to the coming kingdom. You might call this a lowest-common-denominator Christianity.

Catholics and other Christians believe a whole lot more than these propositions. But on these things and a whole lot more all Christians can agree. Any nominal Christian who does not believe these things has no claim to the title "Catholic," no matter what his church affiliation. And any Christian who denies that Catholics who believe these things are brothers and sisters in the faith needs to get out more and meet a few of us.

What does the Catholic Church teach about non-Catholic Christians?

Jesus prayed: "That they may all be one!" (see Jn 17:11, 21-22). "The restoration of unity among all Christians is one of the principal concerns of the Second Vatican Council."[2] The Catholic Church is fully committed to the restoration of visible unity among Christians. Ecumenism "is not just some sort of 'appendix' which is added to the Church's traditional activity. Rather, ecumenism is an organic part of her life and work and consequently must pervade all that she is and does; it must be like the fruit borne by a healthy and flourishing tree which grows to its full stature.... [It is]a duty which springs from the very nature of the Christian community."[3]

I owe much of my Christian life to non-Catholic Christians. Though I was raised Catholic, God used Brethren, Baptist, Anglican, Presbyterian, Pentecostal, and some denominationally indescribable Christians to press the claims of Christ upon me when I was in my early twenties. Largely through them, I came to an adult faith in Christ, a love of evangelism and the Scriptures, and an awareness of the power and guidance of the Holy Spirit.

God's grip on my life has steered my future ever since. My choice of a wife, education, and employment; the manner in which we've raised our children; and eventually even my return to the Catholic Church were all, ironically, deeply influenced by those outside the visible boundaries of the Catholic Church. I even served as an evangelical Protestant pastor for five years, and I still enjoy the friendship and fellowship of many deeply committed non-Catholics.

Many non-Catholics don't realize the degree to which the Catholic Church recognizes them as family even as we insist that Christ willed visible unity for this family. Having loving family members from whom you are separated in significant ways is certainly not unusual in modern culture. But overcoming the separation requires honestly dealing with our "issues."

1. There is plenty of blame to go around for Christian divisions. Those raised as non-Catholic Christians are not guilty of the sin of schism but are to be received as brothers if they believe in Christ and have received a Trinitarian water baptism.[4]

2. Many of the most important building blocks that Christ uses to build up and give life to his Church can exist outside the visible boundaries of the Catholic Church. Non-Catholics have the written Word of God; a life of grace, faith, hope, and charity; the interior gifts of the Holy Spirit; and other important elements. They significantly participate in the drama of salvation.[5]

3. Catholics must appreciate Christ's gifts to non-Catholics, including non-Catholic martyrs. "It is right ... to recognize the riches of Christ and virtuous works in the lives of others who are bearing witness to Christ, sometimes even to the shedding of their blood.... Nor should we forget that anything wrought by the grace of the Holy Spirit in the hearts of our separated brethren can contribute to our own edification."[6]

4. Further, the example of the martyrs, Catholic and non-Catholic, can help us overcome our divisions. "These brothers and sisters of ours, united in the selfless offering of their lives for the Kingdom of God, are the most powerful proof that every factor of division can be transcended and overcome in the total gift of self for the sake of the Gospel."[7]

5. While the Catholic Church has a full deck, its members are often playing with only a few cards. "For although the Catholic Church has been endowed with all divinely revealed truth and with all means of grace, yet its members fail to live by them with all the fervor that they should."[8]

6. We should pray together, learn what each other really believes, avoid erecting unnecessary obstacles by our speech or compromising the faith through a "false irenicism" and cooperate in promoting human dignity and the arts and sciences and in relieving the social afflictions of our time.[9]

7. Christ willed visible unity for his Church. "Nevertheless, our separated brethren ... are not blessed with that unity which Jesus Christ wished to bestow on all those he has given new birth into one body and whom he has quickened to newness of life.... For it is through Christ's Catholic Church alone, which is the universal help towards salvation, that the fullness of the means of salvation can be obtained."[10]

Though we are family, we are not in communion with one another. Fighting has broken out in the family house, and some of the siblings grabbed a few cooking utensils, some family pictures, and some tools and decided to pitch tents in the back yard.

The fatherly authority in the house may have acted a little rashly in telling them to get out. Both sides share the blame, but the truth remains that we are all supposed to be eating at one table in one house and are obligated to seek reconciliation.

After all, we are supposed to bear witness to the world that God has reconciled the world by his Son. As Pope John Paul II asked: "When nonbelievers meet missionaries who do not agree among themselves, even though they all appeal to Christ, will they be in a position to receive the true message?"[11]

Why call yourselves "Catholic" instead of simply "Christian"?

It's not a case of either/or but of both/and. "Christian" was first used to describe the followers of Christ at Antioch. It probably originated among our enemies as a contemptuous nickname (see Acts 11:26; 26:28; 1 Pt 4:16). But by the time St. Ignatius of Antioch wrote in the first decade of the second century, the believers had gladly accepted it.

"Catholic" is simply derived from the Greek word *catholikos,* meaning "universal." We call ourselves Catholic because it describes the scope of Christ's saving mission and the extent of the community he founded. Christ died for the sins of the whole world, and his Church is open to members from every nation, kindred, tongue, region, generation, locale, race, gender, class, and culture. The Catholic Church is the "universal" community founded by Jesus Christ, the Savior of the whole world (see 1 Cor 12:13; Gal 3:28; Col 3:11; Rv 5:9; 7:9; 14:6).

Wonderfully enough, it is St. Ignatius of Antioch who gives us our first recorded use of the term "Catholic" to describe the Church. Ignatius was the second or third bishop of Antioch, a major teaching center in the early Church that had breathed some deep apostolic air. St. Peter had served as bishop just before he went to Rome, and Ignatius was himself mentored by the apostle John.

On his way to martyrdom in Rome, Ignatius left us a body of correspondence that was highly revered in the early centuries of the Church. There he wrote: "You must all follow the bishop as Jesus Christ follows the Father, and the presbytery as you would the Apostles. Wherever the bishop appears, let the people be there; just as wherever Jesus Christ is, there is the Catholic Church."[12]

"Catholic" is not, as many people imagine, a denominational title. It simply describes a quality or mark of Christ's Church.

"Denominationalism," strictly speaking, didn't arise until the breakup of the Western Church in the sixteenth century.

Today the Catholic Church is sometimes referred to as the "Roman Catholic Church." Certain Anglicans, not Catholics, originated the phrase. They wanted to be regarded as the true "Catholics" in contrast to the merely "Roman" Catholics. So they sought to exploit a contradiction in terms. How can one be "Catholic"—that is, universal—and yet merely "Roman" at the same time? It was a clever play on words that was intended as a sneer.

Today we often hear Catholics themselves claiming to be "Roman" Catholic. This is an attempt to turn the tables on the critics and redefine the phrase: "Yes, we are 'Roman' Catholic, meaning that we accept the primacy of Peter and the teaching authority of his successors, who traditionally operate from Rome." These Catholics wear the phrase "Roman Catholic" as a badge of loyalty to Church teaching.

II. Scripture and Tradition

What is Tradition?

When a Catholic refers to "Tradition" or "Sacred Tradition," he is referring to a specific body of unchanging divine revelation. This is different from the "traditions" that include legends, customs, disciplines, or practices that may change from time to time or region to region— for example, to pray facing East or to fast on certain days or to immerse three times during baptism.

Every community has traditions of this latter sort. A family, for example, might have a tradition of not cutting the Thanksgiving turkey until all the relatives arrive. Yet if one year a distant uncle shows up late and people are already seated and enjoying the meal, he may be upset, but he can hardly accuse the family of violating divine revelation.

In a similar way, it's customary for the President of the United States to take his oath of office surrounded by his family and all living presidents. But again, this is a custom, not a matter of divine law. His presidency is not invalidated if he decides to change the tradition.

Sacred Tradition, in contrast, is not simply "doing it the way we've always done it," it is the Word of God. It is divine revelation in both its written form in Scripture and its oral form as teachings passed on from the apostles and carried out in the life of the Church through the centuries. Sacred Tradition, as the *Catechism of the Catholic Church* says, "comes from the apostles and hands on what they received from Jesus' teaching and example and what they learned from the Holy Spirit. The first generation of Christians did not have a written New Testament and the New Testament itself demonstrates the process of living Tradition."[1]

In the New Testament, the Greek word for "tradition" (*paradosis*) is used by both Christ and the apostles with both positive and negative connotations. Christ castigates the traditions of the scribes and the Pharisees that made void the Word of God. On the other hand, he distinguished between true and false tradition and instructed his followers to adhere to the interpretive traditions that did not counter God's revelation (see Mt 15:13; 23:2-3). The apostles typically used "tradition" in a positive way, referring to what they had received from Christ and the Holy Spirit.[2]

The apostles did not plan on passing along divine truth through Scripture alone. When they were faced with conflicts within the local churches, they urged Christians to consult more than the written word. "So then, brethren," insisted St. Paul, "stand firm and hold to the traditions which you were taught by us, either by word of mouth or by letter" (2 Thes 2:15; see also 3:6; 1 Cor 11:2; 15:2-3). Writing was not the only reliable way of passing along the Word of God.

A tremendous amount of material related to the life and teachings of Jesus was contained in the apostles' teaching but didn't make it into the Gospels of Matthew, Mark, Luke, and John. John, for instance, writes: "Now Jesus did many other signs in the presence of the disciples, which are not written in this book; but these are written that you may believe that Jesus is the Christ, the Son of God, and that believing you may have life in his name" (Jn 20:30-31).

John selected the events and sayings from the life of Jesus that would achieve his literary purpose in composing the gospel. But he hadn't exhausted the material. In fact, he declared that the whole world could not contain the books that could be written describing Jesus' life (see Jn 21:25).

When Paul delivered his farewell address to the Ephesian clergy, he noted that he had spent three years with them declaring the "whole counsel of God" (Acts 20:27). Yet we have just a minute portion of this teaching in his letter to the Ephesians, which runs to only six small chapters. During the course of his speech in Acts, St. Paul quoted Jesus saying that "it is more blessed to give than to receive." This quote, however, appears nowhere in Matthew, Mark, Luke, or John. St. Paul was drawing upon the oral apostolic tradition.

The apostolic tradition thus extends beyond what the apostles wrote and was orally passed along by the ordained teachers of the Church. For that reason, the Fathers of the early Church often appealed to "a tradition received from the apostles" to justify certain practices and beliefs.

Where can I find this Sacred Tradition in its fullness?

"The task of giving an authentic interpretation of the Word of God, whether in its written form or in the form of Tradition, has been entrusted to the living, teaching office of the Church alone. Its authority in this matter is exercised in the name of Jesus Christ" (CCC, 85).[3] In Sacred Tradition, Christ continues to teach us through his body, the Church. Jesus did not come to leave us a collection of uninterpreted manuscripts, but rather a teaching community to organically transmit his divine life.

At first blush, many people will shrink from the idea of an authoritative teacher in spiritual matters. I regularly meet with large groups of Catholics and non-Catholics who are interested in discussing the issues that most divide Christians. When we come to the issue of spiritual authority, we play a word association game.

I ask the group to say the first thing that comes into their minds when I say, "authority." Words such as "police," "military," and "boss" predominate. Never has someone said "servant." The responses reveal just how far we are from understanding authority as defined by Jesus and the apostles. In the Christian worldview, authority is a function of servanthood, not a matter of lording it over others. Pope John Paul II, for instance, is called the servant of the servants of God.

The teaching office of the Church is called the Magisterium. This includes the bishops in communion with the successor of St. Peter, the bishop of Rome, the pope. "[T]his Magisterium is not superior to the Word of God, but is its servant. It teaches only what has been handed on to it. At the divine command and with the help of the Holy Spirit, it listens to this devotedly, guards it with dedication, and expounds it faithfully. All that it proposes for belief as being divinely revealed is drawn from this single deposit of faith" (CCC, 86).[4]

The Magisterium proposes no new divine revelation. Public revelation to the Church ceased with the apostles. But the task of passing along the Sacred Tradition, interpreting and applying it to our own day, remains. This is why the New Testament calls the "church of the living God"—not the Scriptures—"the pillar and bulwark of the truth" (1 Tm 3:15).

Can you give me an example of Sacred Tradition not contained in the Bible?

The designation of which books are Scripture—what we sometimes call the "canon of Scripture"—is one example. "Canon" is from a Greek word simply meaning "measuring rod or rule." It's easiest to think of the canon as a ruler or yardstick.

Have you ever wondered why certain books are included in the Bible? Why not others? Who decided? Who had authority to distinguish God-inspired texts from those that were merely edifying, that were doubtful, or that were just plain forgeries? Where did that authority come from? Can it be trusted?

Without an authoritative teaching community, there could have been no closing of the "canon of Scripture"—no one to say decisively, "No other books can be counted as Scripture."

This is significant because people often want to add to or eliminate certain books from the Bible. One of my seminary classmates wanted to replace the Old Testament readings with more contemporary writers such as Dr. Martin Luther King and Thomas Merton. (As committed Christians, King and Merton would have been appalled.) She found these modern writers more meaningful and inspirational than 2 Kings and Leviticus.

For her, a text's inspiration was determined by its relevance and meaning to the individual. The Protestant reformer John Calvin, in his magisterial *Institutes of the Christian Religion,* seemed to hold a similar view: "The word will never gain credit in the hearts of men till it be confirmed by the internal testimony of the Spirit." In other words, we know what is divine Scripture because it attests to itself in our hearts. We feel its power and inspiration over us.

The problem with this view is twofold: First, how many of us feel moved by the Spirit while poring over the animal sacrifice minutiae of Leviticus or tabernacle construction plans in Exodus?

Second, what about the chaos produced when everyone follows his own subjective feelings in pursuit of establishing some public standard of Scripture? Why not include the writings of the "Ascended Masters" channeled by New Age guru Elizabeth Clare Prophet? Why not incorporate the Muslim *Quran* and the Hindu *Bhagavad Gita?* Good heavens! In the 1960s I suppose Khalil Gibran's writings would have been inserted right between the Psalms and Proverbs!

While the Catholic Church teaches the full inspiration and inerrancy of the Bible, inspired Scripture isn't recognized by the mind of the individual but by the mind of Christ operating through his body, the Church.

During the Protestant Reformation a weightier challenge was mounted than that offered by my classmate. Martin Luther rethought the entire canon. He reevaluated seven books of the Old Testament as non-canonical and placed them after the books he considered genuinely "inspired." Among the New Testament books, he criticized Hebrews, James, Jude, and the Apocalypse and removed them from their traditional order, placing them at the back of the New Testament.[5]

He even considered omitting the Epistle of James from the New Testament. "I do not regard [James] as the writing of an apostle," he insisted, because he believed it "is flatly against St. Paul and all the rest of Scripture in ascribing justification to works.... [It is] an epistle of straw ... for it has nothing of the nature of the gospel about it."[6] Nevertheless, he relented and eventually included James in its traditional place in the canon.[7]

In our own generation, a group of scholars associated with the "Jesus Seminar" published a volume called *The Five Gospels*, in which they added the Gospel of Thomas to the New Testament. Such actions press us to ask: Who speaks for the Church? How did we arrive at a closed list of books called Scripture? Who has authority to determine what books should be included in the Bible?

The historical turning points in determining the canon are well known and clear. During the first century the Jews still had an open canon, but when some of the apostolic writings came to be recognized as Scripture along with the Hebrew canon (2 Pt 3:15-16; 1:20), Jewish leaders began closing their list of books. The Church, however, didn't find it necessary to begin composing lists of Scripture until the late second century, when certain heretics created their own lists and carved up the books commonly read in the local churches.

What is a form of Sacred Tradition recognized by all Christians? The very table of contents in our Bibles is a part of Sacred Tradition passed on from the apostles through the Church fathers and to us. The Church did not confer divine inspiration on these books; it simply recognized it. And the Church alone was given the authority to grant such recognition formally and definitively.

An evangelical Protestant friend of mine said to me: "I don't know how you can do it. But if you can come up with the Catholic Church by reading the New Testament, more power to you." My response was, "If you can come up with a New Testament without trusting in the Catholic Church, more power to *you!*" In other words, the argument from Sacred Scripture made against Sacred Tradition saws off the very limb it's sitting on.

Why does the Catholic Bible have more books than the Protestant Bible?

Most simply: Catholics and Orthodox rely on a pre-Christian Jewish list of inspired books. Protestants rely on a post-Christian Jewish list of inspired books. This requires some explanation.

First, we should note that this is unfamiliar territory for a lot of us. When we pick up a Bible we usually want orientation to the great plan of God, and we want to locate our place in it. We hope for a message of love, guidance, encouragement, and consolation. We want sure teaching about life and sturdy standards for living it. In short, we want a word from the living God.

Few of us spend time asking whether St. Paul really wrote Ephesians or whether Job is historical narrative or artful, instructive legend. We rarely ask what criteria the Church employed when it recognized particular books as "inspired"—that is, "God-breathed."

We just accept the volume in our hands, in our pews, or in the top drawer of the Motel 6 bedside table as *the* Bible. We don't check to see if all the books are in there or if some are added. We are rightly assured that any responsible version of the Bible contains the written Word of God and can lead to salvation in Christ (2 Tm 3:16).

Second, all Christian communities agree on the "canonical" twenty-seven books of the New Testament. But what criteria did the Church use to include some books and exclude others?

- Did the writing conform to the "canon of faith"? Here's an important, if little known, historical detail: the word "canon" was never used in the early centuries to mean a closed list of books. "Canon" referred to a way of believing, belonging, and behaving based on the Word of God, which came from the apostles' oral and written teaching.

We can summarize this criterion simply: we know that this writing is true because this is what we do! We don't do these things because they are in these writings; we are already doing these things, thus the writings must be apostolic.

- Was the writing genuinely associated with an apostle? This is the most commonly mentioned test among the early Church Fathers.
- Has it been used in the churches from the beginning?

Arriving at the canon of the New Testament was a communal test of life and experience rather than a formal bureaucratic procedure. Only with Athanasius' Easter letter of A.D. 367 do we finally have a New Testament list that fully corresponds with our current list.

Imagine the two-century-old United States not knowing the full extent of its Constitution and Bill of Rights throughout its entire history. Yet for over 330 years there was no text that functioned as a "constitution" for the Church. Its "constitution" was and is the ongoing, living apostolic authority that Jesus anchored within the community. Other issues aside, Catholics, Orthodox, and Protestants all agree on the extent of the New Testament canon.

Third, Christian communities disagree about the extent of the Old Testament. Protestant Bibles omit at least seven books from the collection of sacred writings that are hallowed by the Catholic and Orthodox Churches.[8]

The omitted seven books are called the "Apocrypha" or the "Deuterocanonicals," meaning "second canon," as opposed to "Protocanonicals," meaning "first canon." The Deuterocanonicals are considered "second" because they are, for the most part, written later than the Protocanonicals. They include Tobit, Judith, 1 and 2 Maccabees, Wisdom of Solomon, Ecclesiasticus (Sirach), and Baruch. Catholic Bibles also contain an additional six chapters (107 verses) in the Book of Esther and another three (174 verses) in the Book of Daniel.

At the birth of the Christian movement, there was no one volume called the "Old Testament." When I was an undergraduate at Michigan State University, the rabbi who taught the Old Testament course regularly elicited chuckles from students when he told them on the first day of class that he didn't believe in the Old Testament. "How can there be an 'Old' Testament," he asked, "when I don't agree there was ever a 'New' Testament? I'm a rabbi. Just let me call it the 'Hebrew Bible.'"

A debate over the number of books in the Hebrew Bible heated up after the rise of Christianity and the split between church and synagogue in the late first century. There was a debate because neither the Hebrew nor Christian Bibles contained a "table of contents." For most Christians and Jews, "The Book" wasn't finished. Even the growing writings of the New Testament didn't set hard boundaries for the extent of the Hebrew Scripture.[9]

Roughly, we had a threefold division: the Law, the Prophets, and the Writings. The "Law" (Torah) was fixed and foundational: Genesis through Deuteronomy. The Prophets were less fixed, since the Jews believed that God had temporarily ceased sending prophets to Israel as a judgment (see 1 Mc 9:27; 14:41). When Messiah would come, a new age of prophecy would begin. The "Writings" portion of Scripture was open, and debate continued over what books really belonged in that collection.

The first Christians were Jews who saw the coming of Christ as the climax of divine revelation. The giving of the promised Holy Spirit generated a final burst of prophecy that became "Scripture" (see 2 Pt 1:21; 3:15-16; 2 Tm 3:16).

Jews who did not regard Jesus as Messiah understandably rejected these "new" Christian writings. They even cast a jaundiced eye toward those earlier accepted "Writings" used by this new sect as they argued their case for Jesus.

For instance, New Testament writers frequently quote from the Septuagint, a third-century B.C. Greek translation of the Old Testament that includes the Deuterocanonicals. While the New Testament never directly quotes the Deuterocanonicals, it often mirrors their thought.[10] Thus the Septuagint grew suspect among many Jewish leaders.

Some argue that since Jesus and the apostles don't directly quote the Deuterocanonicals, they aren't "inspired," that is, "God-breathed," Scripture. But the argument proves too much, for Jesus and the apostles never directly quote from many of the Protocanonicals either. Joshua,

Judges, 1 Samuel, 2 Kings, 1 and 2 Chronicles, Ezra, Nehemiah, Esther, Ruth, Ecclesiastes, Song of Solomon, Ezekiel, Lamentations, Jonah, Obadiah, Nahum, Zephaniah, and Haggai are never quoted, yet all Christians accept these books as "God-breathed."

From the end of the first into the third century, the rabbis debated the status of the Deuterocanonicals as well as some of the Protocanonicals, such as Ruth, Esther, Proverbs, Ezekiel, and the Song of Songs. When they finished, they had rejected the Septuagint and the Deuterocanonicals.

The Church, on the other hand, continued to esteem the Septuagint and used the Deuterocanonicals as Scripture. This is clearly reflected in the Church's ancient practice. For instance:

- From the fourth century until the sixteenth-century Protestant Reformation, the Church used Jerome's Latin Vulgate as its Bible. It included the Deuterocanonicals just as the Septuagint had.
- Church councils at Hippo (393) and Carthage (397, 417) confirmed the consensus of the early Church that the Deuterocanonicals were Scripture.
- In 405 Pope Innocent I reaffirmed the judgment.
- Our earliest Greek manuscripts of the Old Testament contain the Deuterocanonicals.

So how did the Deuterocanonicals get excised? In the sixteenth century, Martin Luther became the first person in history to extract the Deuterocanonicals from their traditional order in Scripture and cluster them after the Protocanonicals. He reasoned that since they supported prayers for the dead and purgatory, they could not be inspired.[11] The Council of Trent, however, reaffirmed the tradition of the early Church and taught that Christians should venerate, love, and obey the Deuterocanonicals just as they did the other Scriptures, for God had authored them.

Why do Catholics believe some doctrines that are not found in the Bible?

We plead not guilty. To the contrary, Catholics do believe that all their beliefs are rooted in Scripture. Some are explicit; others are implicit. Some are obvious; others are obscure.

The Bible is like a nursery garden with plants in varying degrees of maturity. Some biblical truths are like fully developed apple trees ripe with fruit. Everybody can recognize them. Others are like rosebushes just ready to bud. Still others are tiny shoots just breaking through the soil. People may disagree over what will eventually blossom.

Some portions of the Bible are germinating seedbeds whose kernels are barely detectible without a good deal of digging and reflection. But over the course of history, the Holy Spirit rains on this garden, and as the Church continues to tend the plot, it discovers and cultivates some doctrines that may have just started to sprout on the pages of Holy Writ.

One of the glories of the Catholic Church as the Holy Spirit guides it into all truth (Jn 16:12-13) is its capacity to grow in knowledge of Scripture and discover truths from the pages of Scripture that previously were obscure. All formal Catholic beliefs, however, are grounded in the soil of Scripture, and Catholics reject any doctrines that are contrary to Scripture.

Sometimes this growing reflection on the meaning of Scripture is called "development of doctrine." Just as in Scripture we see what theologians call "progressive revelation," we might say development of doctrine is a "progressive understanding of revelation."

For instance, the seed of a doctrine of atonement is planted in Genesis immediately after humanity's original sin. God slays some animals for their skins in order to cover Adam and Eve's nakedness—something of which they've become aware because of their transgression (see Gn 3:8-11, 21). Later the Hebrews are saved from the plague of the death of the firstborn in Egypt when they kill a lamb and cover their lintels with its blood (see Ex 12:1-13). The Law of Moses details further priestly instructions for animal sacrifice to atone for the sins of the people (see, for example, Lv 1:1-17).

Later, the prophets of Israel and Judah begin emphasizing sacrificial obedience as superior to animal sacrifice (see 1 Sm 15:22). They aren't calling for the end of animal sacrifice, but for developing its real intent: Sin is costly, and without obedience to God, even to the point of shedding one's blood, there can be no atonement for sin (see Heb 9:22). When Jesus begins his public ministry, St. John the Baptist presents him as the Lamb of God who takes away the sins of the world. He is obedient to the point of a sacrificial death (see Jn 1:29; Phil 2:8).

In this way, the doctrine of atonement had developed, but it was still true to its origin. You might say that the oak of Jesus' sacrifice was contained in the acorn of animal sacrifice. What was embryonic in Genesis emerged maturely in the Gospels and epistles.

Another way of conceiving how the Church derives doctrines that may at first glance not appear to be in Scripture is to think in terms of logic. The Scripture is a collection of books rich with all kinds of declarative statements that can be divided up between premises and conclusions. Sometimes conclusions are affirmed but the premises are left unstated. Sometimes the premises are stated but the conclusions are not drawn or explicitly stated in the Scripture. As the Church ponders such statements, however, it is fully justified in identifying their logical premises or conclusions and then teaching these as doctrines.

The word *Trinity,* for instance, is nowhere used in the Bible. In fact, the Bible is insistent that there is but one God. The New Testament, however, presents to us three Persons with intelligence and will who are called "God."

The Church grappled with this problem and concluded that there could not be both one God and three gods. This would be a logical contradiction. Therefore, the three divine Persons must subsist as the one God just as one might say six squares subsist as a cube. Of course, God doesn't really have parts, and he is a Being in a class by himself. Nevertheless, the analogy is useful in demonstrating that six of one thing can be one of another. The Three Persons are the one God. Thus we refer to the Triune God who is Father, Son, and Holy Spirit.

Development of doctrine is not a compromise with later conceptions. It simply brings to fruition and maturity what was latent and pregnant. To borrow a phrase from Wordsworth, when it comes to the history of doctrine, "the child is father to the man."

G.K. Chesterton wrote: "When we talk of a child being well-developed, we mean that he has grown bigger and stronger with his own strength; not that he is padded with borrowed pillows or walks on stilts to make him look taller. When we say that a puppy develops into a dog, we do not mean that his growth is a gradual compromise with a cat; we mean that he becomes more doggy and not less."[12]

The Second Vatican Council taught:

The Tradition that comes from the apostles makes progress in the Church with the help of the Holy Spirit.[13] There is a growth in insight into the realities and words that are being passed on. This comes about in various ways. It comes through the contemplation and study of believers who ponder these things in their hearts (see Lk 2:19, 51). It comes from the intimate sense of spiritual realities which they experience. And it comes from the preaching of those who have received, along with their right of succession in the episcopate, the sure charism of truth. Thus, as the centuries go by, the Church is always advancing towards the plentitude of divine truth, until eventually the words of God are fulfilled in her."[14]

Were Catholics ever forbidden to read the Bible? Didn't the Church try to keep the Bible from the people during the Middle Ages?

The simple answer is no. The *Cambridge History of the Bible* answers the charge: "No universal and absolute prohibition of the translation of the Scriptures into the vernacular nor of the use of such translations by clergy or laity was ever issued by any council of the Church or any pope."[15]

It would be nice to just move on with the rest of this book, but I know from long experience that this question is asked because someone has innocently been infected by a bug of half-truth coughed up over a few centuries. I'm sorry you got caught in the spray of an anti-Catholic polemical sneeze. So here goes the unsimple answer.

"Ignorance of the Scripture is ignorance of Christ,"[16] declares the Catholic Church. Thus the Catholic Church has preserved, defended, copied, translated, circulated, and "venerated the Scriptures just as she venerates the body of the Lord.... For in the sacred books, the Father who is in heaven meets His children with great love and speaks with them; and the force and power in the Word of God is so great that it stands as the support and energy of the Church, the strength of faith for her sons, the food of the soul, the pure and everlasting source of spiritual life."[17]

Did the Church during the Middle Ages suppress access to and knowledge of the Scripture? No! Latin was the universal language of the literate, and those who could read at all could read the Latin Vulgate, which was the "vulgar"—that is, the common—translation encouraged and authorized by the Church. For those who couldn't read, there was no pressing need for a vernacular translation. When literacy increased, however, translations quickly emerged in Spanish, Italian, Danish, French, Norwegian, Polish, Bohemian, and Hungarian even before the invention of the printing press.

Translating the Bible into the language of the people did not begin with Martin Luther. Before Luther's monumental German Bible of 1522, Mentelin of Strassburg's translation appeared in 1466. By 1522, fourteen High German and four Low German editions had appeared. Italy and France also had strong traditions of vernacular printing. By the end of the fifteenth century, both Latin Vulgate and vernacular Bible printing had quickly spread through the trade routes.

Scripture in the language of the people has a long Catholic history. In England, Caedmon (died c. 680) and others rendered portions of Scripture into the vernacular. Aelfric (c. 955-c. 1020), the greatest of Old English prose writers, paraphrased Scripture portions into English.

In the sixteenth century, St. Thomas More testified to this long-standing translation tradition: "The whole Bible long before Wyclif's day [1330-1384] was by virtuous and well-learned men translated into the English tongue, and by good and godly people with devotion and soberness well and reverently read." Even the Protestant translators of the Authorized ("King James") Version of 1611 appealed to the common practice of the past in order to justify their own efforts at translation: "So that, to have the Scriptures in the mother tongue is not a quaint concern lately taken up ... but hath been thought upon, and put in practice of old, even from the first times of the conversion of any nation."[18]

Various vernacular versions, then, were available well before the Protestant Reformation.

An oft-repeated charge is that Church leaders went so far as to chain the Bible to the altars so the people couldn't read it. The Church did chain Bibles in this way—but to keep them from thieves, not from the people! Bibles were as valuable as houses, and thieves loved them. We chain telephone books to ensure availability, not restrict access. The Church guaranteed access to the Bible by protecting it.

Certain translations undertaken without the approval of the Church have occasionally been prohibited. The Church was, and is, duty-bound to prohibit incompetent translations. Scripture is not an individual's possession. "Understand this, that no prophecy of scripture is a matter of one's own interpretation.... So also our beloved brother Paul wrote to you.... There are some things in them hard to understand, which the ignorant and unstable twist to their own destruction, as they do the other scriptures" (2 Pt 1:20; 3:15-16).

Love requires that more-educated Christians look out for the less-educated, so the Church must exercise a "quality control" over Scripture translation.

Civil government guards the currency by regulating the mint. When counterfeit bills begin circulating, we expect government action to stop the spread of bogus money. The Church guards the deposit of faith and has a stewardship similar to that of a modern publisher who holds the copyright on a given author's work. She must fulfill her responsibility to insure that the Divine Author's book is not twisted by incompetent or malicious translators.

Great and authoritative voices in the Church have always urged Catholics to intimacy with Scripture.

St. John Chrysostom (344-407): "To become adult Christians you must learn familiarity with the Scriptures."

Pope St. Gregory I (c. 540-604): "Learn the heart of God in the words of God, that you may sigh more eagerly for things eternal, that your soul may be kindled with greater longings for heavenly joys."

St. Bernard of Clairvaux (1090-1153): "The person who thirsts for God eagerly studies and meditates on the inspired Word, knowing that there, he is certain to find the One for whom he thirsts."

Pope Leo XIII (1878-1903): "The solicitude of the apostolic office naturally urges and even compels us ... to desire that this grand source of Catholic revelation [the Bible] should be made safely and abundantly to the flock of Jesus Christ."

Pope St. Pius X (1902-14): "Nothing would please us more than to see our beloved children form the habit of reading the Gospels—not merely from time to time, but every day."

Pope Pius XII (1876-1958): "Our predecessors ... recommended the study or preaching or ... the pious reading and meditation on the sacred Scriptures.... Christ, will men more fully know, more ardently love and more faithfully imitate ... as they are more assiduously urged to know and meditate on the Sacred Letters, especially the New Testament."

Over the centuries, Christ working through his Church has preserved the canon of Scripture, hand-copied the manuscripts, insured the accuracy of translations, and encouraged its reading. So to all people of good will, heed the instruction of Christ—and "take up and read."

III. *Teaching Authority*

What do you mean by apostolic succession?
Does apostolic authority exist today?

"Lo, I am with you always, to the close of the age" (Mt 28:20). The essence of what is called "apostolic succession" is Christ's promise to remain with his Church so that "he who hears you hears me" (Lk 10:16; see also Mt 10:40; Jn 13:20).

People often wish they could have lived during the first century and known Jesus in the flesh. It's a natural aspiration. We want to draw as close to Jesus as possible.

We want to hear his voice instructing us, we want to be nurtured by his love, and we want to be motivated by his power. How can we finite, broken, often sinful men and women hear Christ's voice today as distinctly as the apostles heard it? Did Jesus intend to maintain a living voice today?

I bear Good News: the coming of the Word of God in the flesh represents the closest possible intimacy of God with man. Jesus is called "Emmanuel.... God with us" (Mt 1:23).

While we might say that a deceased loved one is still with us in some sentimental way, Christ is as tangibly present with us as he was in the first century. We are not at a disadvantage to first-century Christians. Jesus is truly alive today and continues his ministry through his body, the Church, speaking and acting with every bit as much authority as he did through the apostles.

Let me put it plainly: he who hears the Church speaking with Christ's authority, hears Christ. He who hears the body, hears the Head. Jesus intended to delegate his authority and ministry to human agents.

Jesus appeared to the apostles after his resurrection and passed his ministry along to them: "As the Father has sent me, even so I send you"

(Jn 20:21). Then he breathed on them, in order to transfer his Holy Spirit, and pronounced, "If you forgive the sins of any, they are forgiven; if you retain the sins of any, they are retained" (v. 23). Jesus is not just handing on the baton or engaging in a legal transaction of authority. He is investing his very life into these men in order that they may pass it along to others.

Even Paul, who claims to have been directly commissioned by Jesus through a vision on the Damascus road, doesn't operate independently but submits his ministry to the twelve apostles. He is set apart for apostolic ministry through the laying on of hands by the leaders of the church of Antioch, who were in communion with the Twelve in Jerusalem (see Acts 13:1-3). In Jerusalem, his ministry is given the apostolic seal of approval, and he continued to plant and strengthen other communities by appointing leaders in every church (see Acts 14:23).

When disputes arose over Paul's preaching, the apostles and elders convened a council in Jerusalem to settle the matter (see Acts 15). Timothy and Titus were extensions of Paul's ministry (2 Tm 2:1-2; Ti 1:5; see also Heb 13:7, 17) and could render judgment on whether or not a particular teaching was apostolic (see 1 Tm 1:3).

Historical connection with the apostles was critical in the early Church. As the gospel was proclaimed throughout "Judea and Samaria and to the end of the earth" (see Acts 1:8), it was vital that the new churches be organically connected with the original apostolic band. Apostles or their delegates were dispatched to strengthen the link with the original Christian community and to verify the authenticity of the new community's faith in Jesus (see Acts 8:14-15; 10:1-48; 11:19-26). Certain teachers lost their legitimacy because they taught without the Church's authorization (see Acts 15:24).

Structured by apostolic authority in this way, the Church was connected with the resurrected life of Jesus not merely by spirit, memory, or preaching, but by direct succession with the twelve apostles, who were the foundation stones of the heavenly Jerusalem, the Israel of God (see Rv 21:12-14).

The Twelve, themselves, demonstrated the importance of apostolic succession when after the suicide of Judas, Peter instructed the other disciples that they must find a successor to Judas' office (see Acts 1:15-26; Ps 69:26; 109:8). "His bishopric let another take." The Greek word here is *episcope*, from which we get "episcopal," or "having to do with a bishop." As one apostle passed away he was replaced by a bishop.

This succession continued after the first century as an essential element by which the original community of Jesus could be identified. Clement of Rome's letter to the Corinthians is considered the most important first-century Christian document outside the New Testament and was widely circulated. He wrote to the church at Corinth around the year 96, while the apostle John may have still been alive.

Pope Clement is not introducing some innovation but rather assuming a way of passing along apostolic leadership when he writes:

Christ ... comes with a message from God and the apostles with a message from Christ.... From land to land, accordingly, and from city to city they preached, and from their earliest converts appointed men whom they had tested by the Spirit to act as bishops and deacons for future believers.... Our apostles, too, were given to understand by our Lord Jesus Christ that the office of the bishop would give rise to intrigues. For this reason, equipped as they were with perfect foreknowledge, they appointed the men mentioned before, and afterwards laid down a rule once for all to this effect: when these men die, other approved men shall succeed to their sacred ministry.

Ignatius, bishop of Antioch (c. 35-110), composed letters to various churches as he was on his way to be martyred in Rome. He wrote:

> All of you are to follow the bishop as Jesus Christ follows the Father, and the elders as the apostles. Respect the deacons as the command of God. Apart from the bishop no one is to do anything pertaining to the Church.... It is not right either to baptize or to celebrate the *agape* [Lord's Supper] apart from the bishop; but whatever he approves is also pleasing to God so that everything you do may be secure and valid. Where the bishop appears, there let the people be, just as where Jesus Christ is, there is the Catholic Church.[2]

If a community lacked this organic, historical connection with the apostles, it couldn't be considered a church: "All are to respect the deacons as Jesus Christ and the bishop as a copy of the Father and elders as the council of God and the band of apostles. For apart from these no group can be called a Church."[3]

Irenaeus, bishop of Lyons (c. 140-202), assumed that Christians possessed the original teaching of the apostles in those communities whose leaders could be traced back to the apostles. This unbroken historical succession guaranteed the integrity and purity of the apostolic tradition. "Anyone who wishes to discern the truth," he insisted, "may see in every church in the whole world the apostolic Tradition clear and manifest. We can enumerate those who were appointed as bishops in the Churches by the apostles and their successors to our own day."[4]

In the Nicene Creed we confess our belief in one, holy, catholic, and apostolic church. For a church to be apostolic, there must be both apostolic teaching and apostolic succession.

Do Catholics believe the pope is the successor of Peter?

Yes. But to grasp the significance of St. Peter's successor we must first appreciate Peter's stature among the twelve apostles. Even the *Evangelical Dictionary of Theology,* a standard Protestant reference book, notes: "Peter's primacy or leadership among the twelve apostles and in the primitive church is now generally accepted by Protestant and Catholic scholars alike."[5]

Simon Peter was a complex, emotional personality—hardly someone you would expect to be given the name *Petros,* that is, "Rock." He was aggressive as a leader, rash enough to try to correct Christ, and cowardly enough to deny him, only to repent and weep bitterly over his sin. On one occasion, his hypocrisy elicited a severe rebuke from Paul (see Gal 2:11-14).

Nevertheless, Jesus chose Peter to fill a role of servant leadership over the others. A simple word count of the Gospels and Acts of the Apostles reveals that Peter is mentioned no less than 195 times—more than all the rest of the Twelve combined. The next most common mention is John, with only 29.

Surely in Peter's life we see the Lord's words vividly illustrated: "My grace is sufficient for you, for my power is made perfect in weakness" (2 Cor 12:9).[6]

Peter's preeminence in Scripture is nicely summed up by Dr. Alan Schreck:

1. In the Gospels, Peter is usually the spokesman for the apostles, especially at climactic moments (Mk 8:29; Mt 18:21; Lk 12:41; Jn 6:67-69).
2. Peter is often the central figure relating to Jesus in dramatic gospel scenes such as walking on the water (Mt 14:28-32; Lk 5:1-11; Mk 10:28; Mt 17:24-27).

3. In the synoptic Gospels, Peter is always named first when the apostles are listed (Mk 3:14-19; Mt 10:1-4; Lk 6:12-16; Acts 1:13). In fact, sometimes the apostles are referred to as simply "Peter and his companions" (Mk 1:36; Lk 9:32; Mk 16:7).

4. In John's Gospel, John waits for Peter before entering Jesus' tomb and allows him to go in first, a sign of honor and respect (Jn 20:3-8). Jesus also singled out Peter as a shepherd of God's people (Jn 21:15-17).

5. Paul lists Peter as the first witness of Jesus' resurrection (1 Cor 15:5), and calls him "Cephas" (rock), the name Jesus gave him (Gal 1:18; 2:9, 11, 14; 1 Cor 1:12; 3:22; 9:5).

6. In the Acts of the Apostles, Peter's leadership is acknowledged in many ways:

   • Peter is the first to proclaim the gospel publicly (Acts 2:14-40)
   • Peter gives many of the major speeches in Acts (Acts 3:12-26; 4:8-12; 5:3-9, 29-32; 8:20-23; 10:34-43; 11:4-18; 15:7-11)
   • The first healing miracle after Pentecost is reportedly worked through Peter's command (Acts 3:6-7), and he apparently had a widely recognized gift of healing (Acts 5:15; 9:34, 38-41).
   • Peter was the first to receive God's revelation that the gospel was to go to the Gentiles (Acts 10:9-48), and he was the first to command the baptism of Gentiles (Acts 10:46-48).[7]

Peter is distinguished from the rest of the Twelve in other Gospel incidents as well. When Jesus revealed that Satan had demanded to sift all of the Twelve, Peter was singled out as the one for whom Jesus was praying. Then Christ prophesied that after his repentance Peter would be the one to strengthen the brethren (see Lk 22:31-32).

Three times Peter boasted that he would never deny Christ (see Mt 26:33-35). Later Jesus matched Peter's boasts with a threefold question: "Do you love me?" Three times Peter answered: "Yes, Lord, you know I do!" Jesus then commissioned Peter to be a good shepherd who would imitate Jesus in laying down his life for Christ's sheep and give them their food in due season (see Jn 21:15-19; see also 10:1-18).

The most telling story, however, illustrating Peter's role in salvation history occurred in the region of Caesarea Philippi, which formed a colorful backdrop for Jesus' words. There the headwaters of the sacred Jordan River originate through an opening in a massive wall of rock approximately two hundred by five hundred feet. The Jews esteemed this spot as a place of revelation in the age to come and as a meeting place for the upper and lower worlds.

Here Jesus said to Peter: "And I tell you, you are Peter [Greek *petros*], and on this rock [*petra*] I will build my church, and the powers of death shall not prevail against it. I will give you the keys of the kingdom of heaven, and whatever you bind on earth shall be bound in heaven, and whatever you loose on earth shall be loosed in heaven" (Mt 16:18-19).

Jesus had just asked the Twelve: "Who do men say that the Son of man is?" (see v. 13). In reply, they tossed out some prominent names from Hebrew history. "But who do you [plural] say that I am?" Jesus asked (v. 15).

Typically, Simon stepped forward and spoke for the apostolic band. He identified Jesus as "the Christ, the Son of the living God" (v. 16). Jesus then turned and identified Simon. "And I tell you, you [singular] are Peter [*petros*], and on this rock [*petra*] I will build my church."

This name change embodies a change in mission. Just as Abram and Jacob were renamed Abraham and Israel when God gave them a new calling (see Gn 17:5; 32:28; 35:10), so it is with Simon Peter.

Abraham became "the rock from which [the children of Israel] were hewn" (Is 51:1). Likewise Peter is the Rock upon which the New Covenant community would be built. As Abraham had spawned a people as numerous as the stars of the heaven and the sands of the sea, so Christ through his agent Peter was to gather a universal people to himself.

It is still common to hear the claim that Jesus promised to build his Church on the rock of a Peter-like faith rather than Peter as a person. But over the last generation an ecumenical team of New Testament scholars reflected a century of deepening research into the languages and background of Matthew's Gospel when they concluded: "[T]here can be no doubt that the rock on which the church was to be built was Peter." As a conservative Lutheran theologian has written: "Nowadays a broad consensus has emerged which—in accordance with the words of the text—applies the promise to Peter as a person."[8]

The now-discredited argument went like this. The Greek text of Matthew contains a pun, a play on words, between *petros* and *petra*. *Petros* refers to a pebble or stone. In contrast, *petra* refers to a massive, immovable rock. Thus, "You are *petros* [a little rock] and upon this *petra* [the big rock of your confession of faith] I will build my church."

Although it is true that *petros* and *petra* can mean little rock and big rock, respectively, in earlier Greek the distinction was largely confined to poetry. By the time Matthew was writing, the distinction was no longer in use. Another Greek word, *lithos*, would have been the proper word to use if Jesus had wanted to contrast a rock with a pebble.

Furthermore, Jesus and the apostles conversed in Aramaic. And in Aramaic, "Peter" and "Rock" are exactly the same word, *Kepha*. "You are *Kepha*, and upon this *kepha* I will build my church." This Aramaic name was carried over into the letters of Paul, who referred to Peter eight times as *"Kepha."*[9]

Then why did Matthew make a distinction at all in the Greek? Because *petra* is a feminine word requiring a feminine ending. Peter, on the other hand, is a male. To call him "Petra" would be like calling Albert "Alberta," Joseph "Josephine," or Rocky "Rockette."

Christ also promised Peter "the keys of the kingdom of heaven." New Testament scholars see Isaiah 22:15 and the following verses as the background for this saying. The words of the two texts have striking parallels.[10]

To understand the import of God's words to the royal steward and his successor in this prophetic passage, we must note first that God had previously promised King David that his royal household would endure forever (see 2 Sm 7:13; Ps 132:11-12). In ancient Israel, the king delegated authority over his house to a chief steward or palace administrator who served as a prime minister in the king's absence. This practice was common in ancient kingdoms. For instance, Joseph had acted as regent, that is, in place of the king (see Gn 41), during Pharaoh's absences.

These keys of the royal establishment were quite literal. The chief steward carried the keys on his shoulder, where they served as a badge of the authority entrusted to him. In the absence of the king, the steward exercised authority in his name through possession of the keys. He also controlled admission to the royal household, the house of David.

Jesus, as David's greater Son, came to fulfill God's promise to David of an eternal kingdom. As he spoke with Peter, he was re-establishing the royal house of David and the fulfillment of the kingdom of Israel based on the twelve apostles (see Rv 21:14). In keeping with the ancient custom, he appointed Peter as the chief steward over the royal household, the Church, and gave him the keys of the kingdom.

Sometimes people will say, "Yes, Peter exercised the power of the keys by opening the kingdom through his preaching (see Acts 2; 8; 10).

At his death, however, the keys were not handed down. The door to heaven was already open."

This position, however, misunderstands the symbolism of the keys. As in Isaiah 22, the keys are passed on. The office of chief steward, by its nature and function, is an ongoing office as long as the King reigns.

When the office is vacated it must be filled, since the work itself continues. Even those Christians not in visible communion with the Catholic Church acknowledge the need for ongoing visible leadership of their Christian communities. When a pastor or bishop dies or resigns, the pastoral office is filled either through election or appointment. The early Church did the same, and the office of Peter, pastor of the universal Church, chief of the apostles, has always been filled.

Jesus used a familiar formula when he told Peter: "Whatever you bind on earth shall be bound in heaven; and whatever you loose on earth shall be loosed in heaven." Those words may sound strange to our ears, but they wouldn't have sounded strange at all to first-century Palestinian Jews. The *Jewish Encyclopedia* explains this phrase as the "rabbinical term for 'forbidding and permitting.'"[11]

The rabbis had the power of "binding and loosing"—that is, of establishing rules of conduct binding on the faith community. They offered authoritative teaching and could excommunicate. To "bind and loose" simply represented the verdict of a teacher of the Law who, on the strength of his expert knowledge of the oral tradition, declared some action or thing prohibited or permitted.

In other words, Peter would give decisions based on the teachings of Jesus. Such decisions would be bound in heaven; that is, honored by God. These powers of binding and loosing were also conferred on the Church generally, but Peter alone was given the keys (see Mt 16:18-19; 18:18).

We must remember that Jesus didn't relinquish his authority to

Peter; he delegated it. Jesus Christ remains the chief holder of the keys (see Rv 1:18; 3:7) just as he remains the Chief Shepherd or Pastor of the Church but delegates his pastoral duties to human beings (see Eph 4:11-13). Upon his return, Peter steps aside.

In the meantime, however, Peter's office continues. This is the role of the pope, the successor of Peter. St. Ambrose, the bishop of Milan whose preaching led to the conversion of St. Augustine, said: "Where Peter is, there is the church." Or as St. Jerome wrote to Pope Damasus: "I follow no one as leader except Christ alone, and therefore I want to remain in union in the church with you, that is, with the chair of Peter. I know that on this rock the church is founded." The Master Teacher who taught us to build our houses on a rock certainly didn't do less than he instructed us to do (see Mt 7:24-27).

Do Catholics really think the pope is infallible?

It's worse than you might think: I'm infallible most of the time. When I say that seven times seven is forty-nine or that Jesus Christ is Lord or that I love my wife, I am speaking infallibly—that is, without error. It's such a modest claim, really, that I even believe you speak infallibly most of the time—and you're coming to this book for answers!

Such a mystique has grown up around papal infallibility that many Christians fail to grasp how unremarkable is the claim. Some might protest that only God teaches infallibly, as though speaking without error is an attribute restricted to Deity. But after all, we assume that most algebra textbooks are without error, and Christians have always believed that God occasionally gifts certain human teachers so they can teach divine truth without error—Matthew, Mark, Luke, and John, to name just a few.

Based on the promises of Christ, Catholics believe that the successor of Peter is, under certain conditions, preserved from teaching falsehood. Vatican I most clearly defined the parameters of this ancient teaching. Vatican II reaffirmed it: "The Roman Pontiff, head of the college of bishops, enjoys this infallibility in virtue of his office, when, as supreme pastor and teacher of all the faithful—who confirms his brethren in the faith (see Lk 22:32)—he proclaims by a definitive act a doctrine pertaining to faith or morals."[12]

The charism of infallibility is restricted to the pope's teaching on faith and morals. If the pope tries to settle a debate over the health benefits of vitamin C or predicts who will win the next Davis Cup or opines on the relative merits of Vivaldi over Handel, we regard his opinion as simply another, hopefully educated, opinion. (I, for one, would argue in favor of Handel.) The pope's competence as pope is restricted to teaching on faith and morals.

Infallibility is also restricted to the pope's exercise of his office as chief human pastor and teacher of the Christian Church. For instance, if the pope is speaking as a private theologian, as John Paul II did in his book *Crossing the Threshold of Hope,* the charism of infallibility doesn't apply.

Sometimes people who don't understand the Church's teaching fear that a pope is free to invent a new doctrine. But papal infallibility doesn't mean that the pope is inspired to bring forth new revelation. He teaches the deposit of faith. He doesn't create it.

When the pope speaks *ex cathedra,* that is, from the chair of Peter, he is only confirming articles of faith embedded in the Sacred Tradition because clarification is needed. He isn't introducing or inventing anything novel. Nobody is less free to innovate than a pope, who is bound by two thousand years of precedent. Infallibility is not a creative gift; it is a protective restriction.

Some popes are also sharper and more effective communicators than others. Papal infallibility doesn't mean that a pope always teaches the right thing at the right time or that he always phrases it as keenly or felicitously as possible. He may fail to emphasize a doctrine at a critical moment in history, and his omission may come to shame future generations. He may be a weak stylist whose syntax and convoluted language fail to resonate with his audience.

Let me bump this up a step. If the pope were given a quiz on faith and morals and circulated it as binding on all Christians, one should hope and expect that he would fill in all the right answers. But infallibility doesn't even guarantee that. It only insures that he won't give the wrong answers. He may not fill in any answers. Critics of papal infallibility, like critics of scriptural infallibility, often fail to appreciate all these limitations on "infallibility."

But what about sinful popes? Yes, and what about sinful apostles? Infallibility doesn't guarantee impeccability (the impossibility of sinning). No Catholic argues that popes are morally unblemished or always act in a manner consistent with their teaching. I understand that Pope John Paul II practices weekly confession.

Paul was forced to withstand Peter to his face when Peter hypocritically refused to dine with Gentile Christians (see Gal 2:11-14). The first pope gave scandal to the teaching that in Christ there was no longer any barrier between Jew and Gentile. He was betraying his own position taken at the Jerusalem Council (Acts 15).

We can imagine Paul thinking: "Of all people, Peter, you should know better." But Paul rebuked Peter for hypocrisy, not heresy.

Catherine of Siena, in her day, confronted the pope over his personal actions. I even thank God that in his providence some of those self-indulgent Renaissance popes were so busy sinning that they didn't have time to do much teaching!

A pope may personally fail to act or teach courageously. But Christ entrusted the office of apostle to weak and sinful men. Even he had his Judas. True to his promise, however, he continues to appoint and assist fallible men so they proclaim his infallible teaching.

How is a pope elected?

While Jesus instituted the office of a universal pastor over the Christian community on earth, he diffused his Spirit within the community, leaving the Church to determine the means of passing along the keys of the kingdom (see Mt 16:17-19). As in so many matters, Jesus didn't come to leave us a rulebook or a bureaucracy, but a Spirit-invested community charged with growing in discernment. Consequently, the means of electing a pope has changed over the two millennia of Christianity in order to assure elections that are spiritually discerned rather than politically calculated.

In the 1968 film *Shoes of the Fisherman,* there's a dramatic moment when all the cardinals rise and spontaneously acclaim their choice of the new pope. Actually, this has never happened. What works for Hollywood rarely works in the real world.

Peter may well have appointed his successor. At other times, the Holy Spirit working through history has used the clergy and the laity to choose the pope. To avoid political influence from ruling families, voting was eventually limited to clergy and then to the College of Cardinals. Cardinals are usually clergy appointed by the Pope as advisors in governing the universal church.

With one exception, since 1179, only cardinals have voted for the pope, and popes are usually elected from among the cardinals. The cardinals can, however, elect whomever they wish as pope as long as he is a baptized male. In 1996 John Paul II issued *Universi Dominici Gregis,* once again updating the rules that govern a papal election.

When a pope dies, a "conclave" is called. A conclave is the fraternal meeting of the cardinals convened to elect a new pope. But it hasn't always been brotherly.

The term conclave comes from the Latin for "locked with a key" and dates back to the time of Pope Gregory X (1272-76). During his election, the cardinals were deadlocked for three and a half years. The laity grew so frustrated waiting for a new pope that they locked the cardinals in session, tore off the roof of the building they were meeting in (to expose them to the elements), and put them on a diet of bread and water until they decided.

Gregory liked the idea and decreed that in the future, cardinals would be locked in one room where they would sleep and vote. After three days their food was limited to one dish a meal. Such severe measures have rarely been necessary, however, and the last conclave to go more than four days was in 1831; it lasted fifty-four days.

During the conclave, the cardinals live within the Vatican in modest quarters assigned by lot. Security is tight. The Sistine Chapel is swept for electronic bugging devices. The cardinals are sequestered and cut off from the outside world. No one can speak to them as they travel between their rooms and the Sistine Chapel.

The conclave begins with prayer and the celebration of the liturgy in the Sistine Chapel. The cardinals swear not to encourage "any group of people or individuals who might wish to intervene in the election of the Roman pontiff." Then follows a meditation on the solemn responsibility of acting "with right intention for the good of the universal Church having only God before their eyes." There are no campaign speeches in the chapel. Any debate goes on outside the chapel.

When the time to vote arrives, each cardinal in secret writes the name of his choice on the ballot in a way that disguises his handwriting. One by one, each cardinal approaches the chapel altar with his folded ballot held up so that it can be seen. After kneeling in prayer for a short time, the cardinal rises and swears, "I call as my witness Christ the Lord who will be my judge, that my vote is given to the one who before God I think should be elected."

Detailed regulations govern the counting of the ballots. Generally, a two-thirds majority is sufficient to elect a pope. After special chemicals are added to the ballots, they are burned so the smoke will be clearly white or black, informing the people gathered in St. Peter's Square and throughout the world whether or not we have a new successor to the apostle Peter. White signals yes; black, not yet. With rare exceptions, those elected pope accept the office and shoulder the new responsibilities asked of them by their brothers.

History shows us that the means for choosing a pope have varied, and the process has sometimes been stormy. But Catholics worship a God who isn't surprised by human frailty and who continues to accomplish his purposes in the world amidst human vacillations. Even the first pope, Peter, who was directly elected by Jesus himself, denied Christ three times and fled him on Good Friday.

Nevertheless, Jesus' promise that the gates of hell will not prevail against his Church is trustworthy. To the amazement of skeptics, the papacy remains the oldest continuing institution in the Western world. It is the "rock" Jesus established (see Mt 16:17-19).

What is a papal encyclical?

Papal encyclicals are, first of all, letters. As such, they continue an ancient tradition. The first Christians enjoyed writing and reading letters. In fact, of the twenty-seven New Testament books, twenty-one of them are letters that were circulated, or "cycled," among the various churches and individuals.

The first pope, the apostle Peter, addressed his first "encyclical" to "the Dispersion in Pontus, Galatia, Cappadocia, Asia, and Bithynia" (1 Pt 1:1). This custom of addressing more than one congregation continued with the successors of the apostles. In the second century, for instance, a letter known as *The Martyrdom of Polycarp* was addressed to "the church of God which sojourns in Philomelium and all dioceses of the holy and Catholic Church in every place."

The bishops of the first centuries frequently sent letters to one another, as well as to the proverbial "people in the pews," in order to teach, encourage, resolve conflict, and foster unity among this new diverse people who were not to be divided by the distinctions of Jew or Gentile, slave or free, rich or poor, educated or uneducated. Since Rome was the political nerve center of the empire and a radiating hub for the spread of the "Jesus" movement, the bishop of Rome received a lot of mail from brother bishops. He was a "networker," a kind of clearinghouse, cycling these letters throughout the network of bishops.

Referring to these early encyclicals, Optatus of Milevis (d. 370) wrote: "Thanks to an exchange of official letters, the entire universe agrees and becomes one with the bishop of Rome in a society of communion." Thus encyclicals were and are important to maintain Christian unity and fidelity to divine revelation.

A *papal* encyclical, then, is simply a teaching letter from the pope, the chief pastor of the universal Church, which addresses matters of doctrine, morals, and discipline or important commemorations. Papal encyclicals are not divinely inspired in the manner of Scripture and do not contain any new revelation. But they are authoritative teaching instruments from the one who teaches in Christ's name and has received a special charism (gift) from the Holy Spirit.

For that reason, a papal encyclical is to be received as possessing authority beyond the personal theological opinion of the pope. Pope Pius XII, in the encyclical *Humani generis* (August 12, 1950), wrote that in a papal encyclical we hear the voice of Jesus. "He who hears you," Jesus said to the apostles, "hears me" (Lk 10:16).

Historically, encyclicals have often been written to solve passing problems, and thus they offer little direct guidance to the questions Catholics face today. Since the practice of sending papal encyclicals was revived in 1740, most of the succeeding 289 encyclicals have passed into history. The use of Islamic names by Christians in Albania or a thank you letter to the American bishops for remembering the pope's anniversary are hardly pressing concerns for contemporary Christians. It's estimated that only about 10 percent of papal encyclicals still provide relevant guidance.

On the other hand, a number of encyclicals address issues of enduring significance. Some of the most important of these would include Pope John Paul II's thirteen encyclicals, which cover matters as diverse as the Church's missionary mandate, the redemption of the human race in Christ, the inviolability of human life, the role of Mary in redemption, Catholic social teaching, the relationship between faith and reason, and the unity of Christians. Other important encyclicals of the last few pontificates include Pope Paul VI's *Ecclesiam suam* (*On the Church*), *Humanae vitae* (*On the regulation of birth*), and *Populorum progressio* (*On the development of peoples*); and Pope John XXIII's *Mater et Magistra* (*On Christianity and social progress*) and *Pacem in terris* (*On establishing universal peace*).

Encyclicals are only one form of official papal documents. These documents can be ranked in the following way based on the degree of formal authority they possess: apostolic constitutions (highest authority), encyclical letters, encyclical epistles, apostolic exhortations, apostolic letters, letters, and messages.

Can a pope resign?

As many as ten popes may have resigned over the centuries, but the historical evidence is ambiguous. Whatever the number, we know that rarely has a pope resigned. The case of Pope Celestine V in 1294 is best known because the poet Dante, in writing the *Inferno,* imagined him to have gone to hell for resigning.

Other bishops must resign at age seventy-five, and the 1983 *Code of Canon Law* (332:2) as well as the regulations established by Pope Paul VI in 1975 provide for the resignation of a pope. But most popes have regarded resignation as out of character for the papal office. One of the chief responsibilities of the pope is to maintain and deepen the unity of God's people, but resigning the office would invite political factions to arise with the hope of pressuring a pope to abdicate. Such a development would violate the very unity the pope is pledged to strengthen.

If a pope becomes disabled through illness, he can delegate much of his work to other Vatican officials. If he goes into a coma, most Vatican offices would continue to operate. Decisions requiring his authority would simply be postponed until his passing and the subsequent papal election. Currently there are no canonical procedures for removing a pope.

We must remember that a pope does not hold political office. He is the earthly household head of the Christian family. And as Pope Paul VI said, paternity cannot be resigned. What could be more unseemly than for the earthly spiritual father of the Christian Church to be a deadbeat dad? It just isn't fitting.

What is canon law?

The Church recognizes many types of law. They are all related, however. All legitimate law ultimately finds its source and justification in the moral character of God, which forms what is called the eternal law. All other legitimate law is an expression of this eternal law and includes natural law, revealed law, civil law, and church law.

Canon law or ecclesiastical law is the official body of laws for the Catholic Church covering faith, morals, and discipline. These laws assist the Church in carrying out her mission to the world and govern the various relationships between persons, offices, and groups within the Catholic communion. Canon law covers such things as how to celebrate the sacraments, administer church property, resolve formal conflicts, and organize official groups such as religious orders and lay associations of the faithful.

While canon law is related to both the natural moral law and revealed law, it is identical with neither. Tenets from both are codified in canon law and are thus unchangeable and universal. Christ's words instituting the Eucharist, for instance, are both divine revelation and part of canon law. These will never change and must be followed everywhere by every priest. But other kinds of canon law are purely disciplinary and subject to change as the Church's needs change or as the culture she is operating in changes.

From the first century, the apostles and the earliest Christian bishops and pastors had to apply divine revelation in particular cultural and social settings. Christ had established a New Covenant that extended beyond the kingdom of Israel. This shift in covenant meant that rabbinic applications of the laws of Moses would be inadequate.

The kingdom of God had been inaugurated. How would these new citizens of the kingdom organize their community upon the new law of Christ? What were the new standards or "canons"? Some of these "laws" would vary from culture to culture.

For instance, the apostle Paul decreed that women must wear head coverings during worship and be silent in the churches (see 1 Cor 11:5-16; 14:34). Perhaps in today's Muslim culture, the original intent of Paul's legislation would be understood and even helpful. But in the modern Western world, these practices no longer bear the meaning they did in the ancient Mediterranean world and could possibly mislead people about the Church's teaching on women.

So some canon law is changeable; some is not. Some canon law applies everywhere, and some is restricted to a particular territory or group.

As the Church grew and exercised the powers of binding and loosing—that is, prohibiting and permitting—promised to her by Christ (see Mt 16:17-19; 18:18), the body of church orders, liturgical procedures, council canons, and so on also grew. In the mid-twelfth century, the scholarly monk Gratian collected and organized four thousand council decrees, papal pronouncements, and texts from the Church fathers in a single work called the *Decretum Gratiani.*

For his labors, he came to be called the "father of canon law," and the Italian poet Dante happily assigned him a place in Paradise. Gratian's text came to form the first part of the *Corpus Iuris Canonici* (Body of Canon Law), which remained the standard collection until the first full-scale Code of Canon Law was issued in 1917.

When Pope John XXIII announced his intention to call the Second Vatican Council in 1959, he also announced a new revision of canon law, which was completed in 1983. This law governs the Western Catholic Church. There is also the Code of Canons of the Eastern Churches, which was completed in 1990.

Only a pope or an ecumenical council has the authority to create canon law or interpret it for the universal Church. The Pontifical Commission for the Authentic Interpretation of the Code assists the Pope by fielding inquiries about canon law, proposing correct interpretations, and then sending them to the pope for final approval. The legal system of the Catholic Church is the oldest such system continually operating in the world.

What was Vatican II?

The Second Vatican Council (also called Vatican II) was held from October 11, 1962, to December 8, 1965. It was the twenty-first ecumenical ("whole world") council of the Catholic Church and certainly the single most important event for the Catholic Church in the twentieth century. Without question, it has set the tone and agenda for the Catholic Church ever since.

An ecumenical council is a solemn, official gathering of all the bishops of the world and, when confirmed by the successor of Peter (the pope), constitutes the highest teaching authority within the Church. Catholics believe these councils are guided by the Holy Spirit in a special way and are preserved from error.

The prototype for ecumenical councils is the Jerusalem Council, which convened around the year 49 or 50 and is described in Acts 15. Disputes had broken out among Christian teachers and evangelists over the conditions by which Gentile believers should be received into the Church. The disagreements had become so sharp that the unity of the Church was threatened. So the apostles and bishops gathered in Jerusalem, imploring the special guidance of the Holy Spirit to resolve the problem.

After prayer and debate, the issue was settled. A document was produced declaring the decision. Believers throughout the world were to regard the decision of the apostles and bishops as authoritative. The unity of the Church had been preserved.

Nearly nineteen hundred years after the Jerusalem Council, Vatican II was opened in 1962 by Pope John XXIII. Over twenty-six hundred bishops attended, with many other Catholic and non-Catholic observers. Overall participation exceeded three thousand. After the death of John XXIII, the Council was continued by Pope Paul VI, who succeeded him on June 21, 1963.

The Council was convened to foster unity among Christians, renew the Church, and update some of its forms and institutions, as well as promote peace and the unity of all mankind. It sought to pass along faithfully the sacred truths of the faith, but with a view towards teaching it more effectively in the modern world. As Pope John XXIII put it: "The substance of the ancient doctrine is one thing, and the way in which it is presented is another."

Unlike many previous councils, Vatican II wasn't convened for the purpose of combating heresy or to resolve some threat to divide the Church. It did, however, produce sixteen documents with a number of distinct emphases:

- The Church is, first and foremost, a mystery or sacrament and is more than the visible institution.
- While the fullness of the faith subsists in the Catholic Church, all baptized Christians are brothers and sisters already in some imperfect communion with the Catholic Church.
- Our first step towards unity is personal renewal and repentance: "There can be no ecumenism worthy of the name without a change of heart.... Let all Christ's faithful remember that the more purely they strive to live according to the gospel, the more they are fostering and even practicing Christian unity."[13]

- The laity, the people of God, are called by God to extend the mission of the Church especially in areas of evangelization, social justice, family life, the media, and the development of a more humane culture.
- Worship requires the "full, conscious, active participation" of all the lay faithful since the Eucharistic liturgy represents the source and summit of our faith.
- We must have a renewed study of Sacred Scripture. "Just as the life of the Church grows through persistent participation in the Eucharistic mystery, so we may hope for a new surge of spiritual vitality from intensified veneration for God's word, which 'lasts forever' (Is 40:8; 1 Pt 1:23-25)."[14]
- Since faith is a free act and cannot be coerced, all people by virtue of their created dignity as the image of God have a right to religious liberty.
- God is often at work in other world religions. Dialogue with non-Christians is essential. The call to dialogue, however, does not mute the call to conversion. The Catholic Church is a missionary Church, and every disciple of Christ is obligated to see himself as a missionary according to his gifts and abilities.
- Religious life must be renewed by a fresh discovery of the gospel, which engenders new forms of religious life.

As a result of the Council, Catholic Scripture study has increased and a renewed liturgy has been installed. The laity has assumed a more prominent place in guiding parishes, proclaiming the gospel, and serving the poor and the unborn. Various renewal movements have flourished. Catholics find themselves in prayer groups, Bible studies, and social reform work with many Christians outside the Catholic Church.

High-level ecumenical dialogues have produced much better

formal relations between the Catholic Church and other Christian communities. Pope John Paul II has come to be admired as a leading advocate for religious liberty, peace, the poor, and refugees.

At the same time, much internal debate, even controversy, has ensued in the wake of Vatican II, especially over liturgy, ecumenism, and catechesis. But what would one expect from a Council that sought to maintain firm continuity with eternal truths yet risked updating its methods in proclaiming that truth?

There has also been a stunning decline of priests and nuns since the Second Vatican Council. Why? Many are the proposed answers. Am I whimsical to think that it is the Holy Spirit's way of prodding the laity to take responsibility for Christ's Church? The Church is far broader than its leadership.

Occasionally, among Catholics usually in debate with one another, you will hear puzzling references to the "spirit of Vatican II." My suggestion? Read the text of Vatican II before trying to discern its spirit. The Spirit and the Word are one.[15]

What is the *Catechism of the Catholic Church?*

In 1992 the first universal *Catechism of the Catholic Church* in over four hundred years was completed. Two years later it was published in English. It had been prepared through six years of intense work by a papal commission consisting of twelve cardinals and bishops.

The word "catechism" comes from the Greek word *katekhein,* meaning "to resound, to echo, to make [one] hear." In the New Testament, *katekhein* refers to instruction in the way of the Lord. A disciple is a learner, that is, one instructed by the master with the aim of becoming like him (see Lk 6:40).

Christ is the Master who instructs us through his body, the Church. A catechumen is the person undergoing instruction in the faith. To catechize is to instruct; catechesis is the instruction. A catechism "echoes" those instructions and is a compilation of basic Christian truths to be used to instruct disciples and guide teachers.

In Scripture we occasionally see brief creeds and teaching summaries, but our earliest systematic presentation of Christian doctrine for new converts is the *Didache,* a text from the late first century. Examples of fourth-century catechetical instruction can be found in St. Cyril of Jerusalem's *Lectures,* St. Gregory of Nyssa's *Catechetical Oration,* and St. Augustine's *De Catechizandis Rudibus.*

Catechetical materials varied from region to region and were not uniform. The invention of the printing press and, later, the Protestant Reformation changed this. With the teaching of the Church under attack, it was necessary to standardize the instruction.

The first catechism intended for universal distribution and use was commissioned by the Council of Trent and issued by Pope St. Pius V in 1566. It is commonly called *The Roman Catechism.* In the United States a national catechism was produced in the late nineteenth century based upon the Roman Catechism; it was called *The Baltimore Catechism.*

After the Second Vatican Council (1962-65), the need for a clear restatement of basic Catholic teaching began to be felt. In 1985, the bishops of the Catholic Church recommended to Pope John Paul II that a new universal catechism be composed. After much consultation with theologians and the bishops, the *Catechism of the Catholic Church* was issued in 1994, directed to the bishops, all teachers of the faith, the Christian faithful, and all sincere inquirers.

Pope John Paul II has described this new catechism as "a sure and authentic reference text for teaching Catholic doctrine and particularly for preparing local catechisms. It is also offered to all the faithful who wish to deepen their knowledge of the unfathomable riches of salvation (cf. Eph 3:8). It is meant to support ecumenical efforts that are moved by the holy desire for the unity of all Christians, showing carefully the content and wondrous harmony of the Catholic faith. The *Catechism of the Catholic Church,* lastly, is offered to every individual who asks us to give an account of the hope that is in us (cf. 1 Pt 3:15) and who wants to know what the Catholic Church believes."[16]

For someone interested in pursuing what the Catholic Church actually teaches, rather than being tossed to and fro by the opinions of various Catholics, the *Catechism of the Catholic Church* is the place to start. Millions are now in circulation, and it is easily available at most bookstores.

IV. *Salvation*

Are Catholics trying to work their way to heaven?

It cannot be said too strongly: We do not earn our salvation. "For the wages of sin [what we earn] is death, but the free gift of God [what we do not earn] is eternal life in Christ Jesus our Lord" (Rom 6:23). Again, we "inherit the kingdom"; we don't earn it.[1] An unknown rich uncle may leave me an inheritance, but nothing I have done obligates him to bequeath me a fortune. It is a gift.

This gift, objectively speaking, is the redemption won by Christ's sacrificial death. The Son of God became man so that men might once again share in the life of God. "For God so loved the world that he gave his only Son, that whoever believes in him should not perish but have eternal life" (Jn 3:16).

This is the good news Christ commanded us to preach. "Go into all the world and preach the gospel to the whole creation. He who believes and is baptized will be saved" (Mk 16:15-16). Christ's death is sufficient for the sins of the whole world.

Yet subjectively speaking, how is Christ's sufficient sacrifice made efficient and actual in our lives? St. Paul tells us: "Work out your own salvation with fear and trembling" (Phil 2:12). Wait a minute! Is God giving us a free gift in one hand only to snatch it back with the other? Is he like a cruel parent who promises good gifts to his children but then forces them into fearful labor to claim them?

Not at all. Listen to St. Paul again. "Work out your own salvation with fear and trembling; for God is at work in you, both to will and to work for his good pleasure" (Phil 2:12-13).

The gift of salvation is the very life of God. We are to become "partakers of the divine nature" (2 Pt 1:4). This is good news to people overwhelmed by the world's cares and injustices, drowning in the undertow of their and the world's disordered passions.

The gospel is not God calling from the west bank of the river, "Swim harder, try harder." The good news is that God himself has jumped into the river, is giving us mouth-to-mouth resuscitation, embracing and guiding us as we swim back to holy ground. God himself is the gift, indwelling us, motivating us by his grace, empowering us by his Spirit so that we may lay claim to all that we have inherited.

Paul, often called "the apostle of God's grace," sees no contradiction between grace-filled human exertion and salvation as a free gift. "But by the grace of God I am what I am, and his grace toward me was not in vain. On the contrary, I worked harder than any of them [the other apostles], though it was not I, but the grace of God which is with me" (1 Cor 15:10).

So the Catholic Church doesn't teach salvation by *works* but rather, to use St. Paul's phrase, salvation by *grace* through faith working in love (see Gal 5:6). The faith that brings us into right relationship with God and makes us adopted sons and daughters of God is also a working faith. Paul calls it "the obedience of faith" (Rom 1:5; see also 16:26; Acts 6:7; 1 Thes 1:3).

Rather than recap the swirling centuries-old debate over the relationship between faith and works, let's just listen carefully to Paul as he describes his own spiritual trajectory towards heaven. How did he live out salvation by faith working in love?

[T]hat I may know him and the power of his resurrection, and may share his sufferings, becoming like him in his death, that if possible I may attain the resurrection from the dead. Not that I have already obtained this or am already perfect; but I press on to make it my own, because Christ Jesus has made me his own. Brethren, I do not consider that I have made it my own; but one thing I do, forgetting what lies behind and straining forward to what lies ahead, I press on toward the goal for the prize of the upward call of God in Christ Jesus.... Brethren, join in imitating me, and mark those who so live as you have an example in us.

PHILIPPIANS 3:10-14, 17

Did St. Paul in his striving fail to rely on the sufficiency of Christ's atoning death? He obviously didn't think so. In one passage he even used language that some Christians today might regard as a reckless undermining of the adequacy of Jesus' work on the cross: "Now I rejoice in my sufferings for your sake, and in my flesh I complete what is lacking in Christ's afflictions for the sake of his body, that is, the church" (Col 1:24).

Unfazed by the debates to come fifteen hundred years later during the Protestant Reformation, Paul didn't fear being misunderstood. In being united with Christ's sufferings he was making Christ visible for the redemption of the world. The same Jesus who suffered on the cross was living his life through St. Paul.

"I have been crucified with Christ," he declared. "It is no longer I who live, but Christ who lives in me" (Gal 2:20; see also Rom 6:3-8; 8:12-17; Col 3:1-4; Eph 2:5-6). Like a birthing mother, he longs for all Christians to manifest this same Christ: "My little children, with whom I am again in travail until Christ be formed in you!" (Gal 4:19).

"Straining forward to what lies ahead ... continuing pursuit of the goal ... filling up what is lacking in Christ's afflictions ... again in labor until Christ be formed ..." God's grace enables us to exert ourselves in order to actualize full salvation. We are called to become strenuously all that God has called us to be: saints (see Rom 1:7; 16:15; 1 Cor 1:2; 2 Cor 1:1; Eph 2:19).

This should give pause to anyone who claims to possess already fully what is not yet fully realized. We don't cross the finish line in our race for salvation until we stand face to face with God for all eternity and hear him say, "Well done, good and faithful servant."[2]

It's common for some Christians to profess that we are "justified [that is, made right with God] by faith alone." Much polemical ink has been spilled in this dispute. But the phrase doesn't appear in Christian history *in its Protestant meaning* until the sixteenth century.[3] We should also realize that the only passage of Scripture where the expression "justified by faith alone" appears is James 2:24, in which we are told that we are "*not* [justified] by faith alone" (emphasis added). If our faith doesn't bring forth good deeds, St. James tell us, then our faith is not saving faith.

But while Christians aren't saved by works in themselves, they will be judged according to them. At the close of his revelation to St. John, Jesus promised, "Behold, I am coming soon, bringing my recompense, to repay every one for what he has done" (Rv 22:12).[4]

Again, how can this be? How can we be saved by grace but judged by our works? Because the grace to believe in Christ is the grace to obey God. Faith is made complete by expressing itself in action (see Jas 2:14-26; 1 Thes 1:3). Works are crystallized faith. As Jesus said, "If you love me, you will keep my commandments" (Jn 14:15; see also 1 Jn 2:3). And his commandments are not burdensome (1 Jn 5:3; see also Mt 11:30); we need only pray as St. Augustine prayed: "Command what you will, and give what you command."

God created us in his image and likeness to rule as co-regents of his creation. We were created for good works (Gn 1:27-28; Eph 2:8-10). His purpose in redeeming us isn't different from his purpose in creating us. Grace builds on nature.

Consequently, it's misleading to say that we are working to get to heaven. More accurately, we are given the gift of salvation so that we might fulfill our natures. Thus we are commanded to "not grow weary in well-doing" (Gal 6:9).

People cannot absolutely deserve any rewards from God (see CCC,

2007). But in God's gracious plan of redemption, he invites us to receive his gift of eternal life and become his friends who love and labor with him freely. If we do anything noble and virtuous it is because he, in his mercy, empowers us to perform such good works.

When we flourish in our efforts, he blesses us with eternal union with him. As the theologian and catechist Fr. Ronald Lawlor puts it: "We are said to merit eternal life, then, because we freely do the saving deeds that God makes it possible for us to do. But all is in the context of grace. 'When God crowns our merits,' St. Augustine remarks, 'is he not crowning precisely his own gifts?'"

Why do Catholics believe they can lose their salvation?

Because it is too easy to be a Christian—or even a Hindu or a Muslim or a Jew—in name only. Any "believer" can fail to live a life that corresponds with what he claims to believe. It's a universal human problem.

We often deceive ourselves about our ultimate commitments and must strive to bring our actions in line with our beliefs. While we all recognize how presumptuous it is to judge another person's standing with God, it may be equally presumptuous to judge our own final status with God. He is the ultimate Judge; we are not.

Call it the problem of nominal Christianity, minimalism, dead faith, or believing in vain, it has long been a chronic problem for the people of God. Scripture urges us to live in such a way that we're prepared for the final judgment, as the outcome, even for believers, is not entirely certain.

Jesus warned his disciples:

Every tree that does not bear good fruit is cut down and thrown into the fire.... Not every one who says to me, "Lord, Lord," shall enter the kingdom of heaven, but he who does the will of my Father who is in heaven. On that day many will say to me, "Lord, Lord, did we not prophesy in your name, and cast out demons in your name, and do many mighty works in your name?" And then I will declare to them, "I never knew you; depart from me, you evildoers.

MATTHEW 7:19, 21-23; see also 1 CORINTHIANS 4:1-5

The prophet Malachi also speaks of judgment as a day when "once more you shall distinguish between the righteous and the wicked, between one who serves God and one who does not serve him" (Mal 3:18). Our salvation isn't fixed by once "accepting Christ as our personal Savior." It's made certain by continuing to obey him lovingly as our Lord. "Faith apart from works is dead" (Jas 2:26).

Oftentimes the new believer starts off enthusiastically sharing his newfound faith, confessing Jesus before men, doing good works, and uprooting the weeds of sin that have grown up in his life—only, in time, to grow weary and indifferent. Why? Jesus gives us one reason: "As were the days of Noah, so will be the coming of the Son of man. For as in those days before the flood they were eating and drinking, marrying and giving in marriage, until the day when Noah entered the ark, and they did not know until the flood came and swept them all away, so will be the coming of the Son of man" (Mt 24:37-39; see also Lk 12:8-9).

What is the great wickedness that deadens people to God? We can be lulled into spiritual indifference by the normal rhythms of innocent secular pursuits. "Eating and drinking, marrying and being married," the basic rituals of everyday life, can anesthetize us so we ignore living in light of eternity and the coming judgment.

The people described here weren't preoccupied with consciously doing evil. They had simply grown tepid toward God. Sadly, this spiritual numbness afflicts Christians as well. Jesus warns the church at Laodicea: "I know your works: you are neither cold nor hot. Would that you were cold or hot! So, because you are lukewarm, and neither cold nor hot, I will spew you out of my mouth" (Rv 3:15-16).

We must keep the engine of our spiritual life warm to God and continually motor our lives guided by his will. Why do Catholics believe we can lose our salvation? Because even God won't steer a parked car!

The ongoing work of God in redeeming us requires our ongoing free cooperation. As St. Augustine said: "The God who created us without our participation has not willed to save us without our cooperation." Until the process of salvation is complete, we can freely opt out of it by refusing God's grace and sinning mortally.

Some evangelical Protestants deny that salvation can be surrendered. It's a doctrine commonly called "eternal security."5 But most Christians throughout history have believed otherwise: the Eastern Orthodox; the Anglicans and Episcopalians; those in the Wesleyan tradition such as the Methodists, Pentecostals, Nazarenes, and the Holiness churches; many Episcopalians; the descendants of the Anabaptists, such as the Mennonites, Brethren, Quakers, and Amish—all these join Catholics in recognizing the tragic possibility that a person once in right relationship with God can sever and forfeit that relationship.

Even St. Paul, who had as dramatic and undeniable a conversion as can be imagined (see Acts 9:1-21; 22:1-16; 26:1-18), did not regard his own ultimate salvation as absolutely assured. Exertion was necessary. Using imagery from the Greek gymnasia and athletic games, he wrote:

Do you not know that in a race all the runners compete, but only one receives the prize? So run that you may obtain it. Every athlete exercises self-control in all things. They do it to receive a perishable wreath, but we an imperishable. Well, I do not run aimlessly, I do not box as beating the air; but I pommel my body and subdue it, lest after preaching to others I myself should be disqualified.

1 CORINTHIANS 9:24-27

Even after the divine Word impregnates us, so to speak, it's still possible that our salvation will be stillborn. "Now I would remind you, brethren," warned the apostle Paul, "in what terms I preached to you the gospel, which you received, in which you stand, by which you are saved, if you hold it fast—*unless* you believed in vain" (1 Cor 15:1-2, emphasis added).

What an awful possibility! To receive the gospel, embark upon the journey of salvation ("being saved"), and yet, ultimately, to have "believed in vain" (see also Heb 6:4-12; 10:26-39; Jas 2:26).

Paul wept over one example of this possibility: his kinsmen, the Jews of the first century. In spite of having received a divine calling and election, the covenants, the law, the oracles of God, the promises, the temple, they still largely rejected their Messiah (see Rom 9:1-9; 11:11-24). Drawing upon the history of ancient Israel's wandering in the wilderness, Paul illustrated the danger of taking God's love and mercy for granted, concluding: "Therefore, let any one who thinks that he stands take heed lest he fall" (1 Cor 10:12; see also Gal 5:19-21; 6:7-10).

Even after we're born again through faith and baptism, we retain our free will and an inclination to sin. Thus we can still choose to turn our backs on God. It is not unlike my marriage. I know that I am married and love Sally and am confident of her continuing love for me. However, I can break the relationship through unfaithfulness. I can walk away from her.

Would that mean that we were never really married or that I never really loved her? No, it would mean that I failed to grow in my love. Instead of nurturing the relationship, I let it wither. As the bumper sticker says, "If God seems far away, guess who moved?"

So even though we are presently infused with the life of the age to come, mortal sin can extinguish the flame of divine life (sanctifying grace) within us. Thus the Scripture urges us to endure to the end, vigilantly watching for Christ's return, diligently stewarding the Master's resources and caring for the sick, imprisoned, and needy just as did the wise virgins, the faithful servant, and the sheep described in the parables of Matthew 25 (see also Mt 13:40-43; 24:45-51; Mk 13:32-37; Rv 2:10, 25, 26). These exhortations to remain faithful to the end would be meaningless if our ultimate salvation were inevitable.

Advocates of "eternal security" do us a service, however. They magnify those passages that remind us how God protects those who are his: "No one shall snatch them out of my hand" (Jn 10:28).

Who shall bring any charge against God's elect? It is God who justifies; who is to condemn? ... Who shall separate us from the love of Christ? Shall tribulation, or distress, or persecution, or famine, or nakedness, or peril, or sword? ... No, in all these things we are more than conquerors through him who loved us. For I am sure that neither death, nor life, nor angels, nor principalities, nor things present, nor things to come, nor powers, nor height, nor depth, nor anything else in all creation, will be able to separate us from the love of God in Christ Jesus.

ROMANS 8:33-34, 35, 37-39

It's impossible to get beyond God's loving reach. But even though love woos the will, it can be spurned. For God to force himself upon us would not be love; it would be spiritual rape. Love presupposes cooperation.

Do Catholics then perpetually worry and anguish over their spiritual state? No, we live in hope, "the confident expectation of divine blessing and the beatific vision of God" (CCC, 2090). Like St. Paul, "we rejoice in our hope of sharing the glory of God" (Rom 5:2) and know that "for in this hope we were saved" (Rom 8:24).

But hope is always directed toward the future. If we fully possess what we hope for, then hope is unnecessary. "Now hope that is seen is not hope. For who hopes for what he sees? But if we hope for what we do not see, we wait for it with patience" (Rom 8:24-25).

We thank St. John for writing so that "our joy may be complete ... that you may *know* that you have eternal life" (1 Jn 1:4; 5:13, emphasis added). We also thank him for telling us how we know: "And by this we may be sure that we know him, if we keep his commandments" (1 Jn 2:3).

Catholics have a moral assurance of salvation, not an absolute assurance. As we "walk in the light, as he is in the light, we have fellowship with one another, and the blood of Jesus his Son cleanses us from all sin" (1 Jn 1:7).

As we cooperate with the grace of God, we are being transformed into the saints that he created us to be. Jesus' atonement is the source of our hope, and as he put it, "no one who puts his hand to the plow and looks back is fit for the kingdom of God" (Lk 9:62). We trust that as God enables our hand to grip the plow, he is making us fit for the kingdom of God. Of that Catholics are assured.

Do Catholics still believe in mortal sin?

Mortal sin is a tragic possibility for human beings. It destroys love in our hearts through a serious violation of God's law. It turns us away from God, who is our ultimate end (see CCC, 1854-64).

Occasionally we hear fellow Christians say, "Little sins, big sins, all sins are alike in God's eyes." But God doesn't weigh all moral matters equally. To sin against a greater good is to commit a greater evil. Scripture itself testifies to greater and lesser sins.[6]

When Jesus taught "that every one who looks at a woman lustfully has already committed adultery with her in his heart" (Mt 5:28), he wasn't suggesting that it is just as bad to think it as to do it. Lust is not adultery. It's adultery in one's heart. Sin springs from the heart. To commit it with one's body is even a worse sin, for it has social consequences that mental lust does not.

As I wrote earlier, the Bible is like a lush garden with a germinating seedbed surrounding it. Some of the vegetation is fully mature and ripe. Some is ready to blossom. Some is just beginning to sprout. As the Catholic Church is guided by the Holy Spirit into all truth (see Jn 16:12-13) it can afford to take seriously those subtle distinctions in Scripture often ignored by other Christian traditions and actually give them theological, even institutional, expression.

So it is with a mysterious passage in 1 John 5:16-17: "If any one sees his brother committing what is not a mortal sin, he will ask, and God will give him life for those whose sin is not mortal. There is a sin which is mortal; I do not say that one is to pray for that. All wrongdoing is sin, but there is sin which is not mortal."

Scripture recognizes at least two different classes of sin. A mortal sin is deadly inasmuch as it destroys the life of God within us. While all sin misses the mark of God's will, not all sin is mortal. As with our physical bodies, all illness wounds, but not all illness is fatal. So too with sickness of soul: some diseases are lethal, others only maim and scar. All need healing.

To resurrect the soul that's been strangled by deadly sin requires some special antidote of God's mercy beyond the prayers of the community. This will lead us to Christ's constant offer of forgiveness in the sacrament of penance, which we'll discuss later.

God has revealed to us the nature and destiny of man. He calls us beyond the development of our intelligence, physique, wealth, family, or art. We are called to a supernatural elevation of our being that surpasses all our original created endowments. We are made for more than this world. We are called to be sons of God and to share in the divine life itself. This is the good news.

"But to all who received him, who believed in his name, [Jesus, the true light that has come into the world], he gave power to become children of God; who were born, not of blood nor of the will of the flesh nor of the will of man, but of God" (Jn 1:12-13; see also 1:9; 1 Jn 3:2)

"[H]e has granted to us his precious and very great promises, that through these you may escape from the corruption that is in the world because of passion, and become partakers of the divine nature" (2 Pt 1:4; see also Heb 12:10).

We are invited to become partakers of the divine nature. For those who have received eternal life, God's very life is coursing through their souls. He intends and has already begun to raise us to a new sphere of existence where we participate in the intimate love and communication of the Trinity (see Jn 14:15-21; 15:1-17, 26-27; 16:12-15; 17:20-26).

This reality staggers the imagination and begs for illustration.

Have you ever had a dearly beloved pet? Your beautiful black Labrador retriever, Ben, is gentle around the children, faithful to his master, amusing in his chasing of rabbits, and trained to fetch. He loves to lie on your feet as you sit before the fireplace rocking for hours on end.

Ben is ordered to his natural end—that is, he is all that a dog was naturally made to be. You know him and he knows you. Well, we should say that you know him as a master knows a pet, and he knows you as a pet knows a master.

But imagine that one balmy Saturday evening you and a friend are about to enjoy some chess. He opens and plays white pawn to king four. Ben, watching with one sleepy eye open, rises on his haunches from in front of the fireplace, reaches a paw across the board, and plays black knight to king bishop three.

You gasp. You glare. You say, "What are you doing? Bobby Fischer played that gambit in Buenos Aires against Boris Spassky and got his head ripped off." Ben leans over and whispers, "Yes, but six months later, he psyched Spassky out by playing the same unsound move. Spassky lost his nerve. Match to Fischer."

You then wake up from your chess coma and realize what's going on. After you've finished doubting your sanity, you would say, "Ben's entered another order of being; the human life has taken hold of him. He now knows as he has been known."

This scenario strains credulity. But in a small way it points to the startling kind of change God intends for us mortal creatures. He wants to raise us up and confer his divine life on us so that we know him as he knows us (1 Cor 13:12).

By turning us away from God, mortal sin breaks our growing intimacy with our Father. Our freedom to spit in God's face is both our glory and our tragedy. Moral choice and responsibility elevate us above the lower primates. The primates' apparent choices may be conditioned; we have the power, however, to make choices that set us on a trajectory that can lead to eternal union with God or eternal separation from him.

So what are the mortal sins? The Church doesn't anywhere keep an exhaustive list. Nor can they be tallied from isolated passages of Scripture. This is because part of what determines a mortal sin is the interior state of the one sinning.

"For a sin to be mortal," the *Catechism* declares, "three conditions must together be met: Mortal sin is sin whose object is grave matter and which is also committed with full knowledge and deliberate consent" (CCC, 1857).[7] What is "grave matter"? It includes anything so serious that it would cause us to be separated from God or the communion of the Church.[8]

If I knowingly and deliberately offend God in a serious matter, I forfeit my share in the divine life, and my trajectory to heaven is thrown off course and toward separation from him. I'm headed for hell. How can I make a course correction and restore the divine life within me? I can't—but Christ has offered to do it for me in the sacrament of penance. (See "Why do Catholics confess to a priest?")

Do Catholics still believe in purgatory?

If by "purgatory" we mean a second chance after death for repentance, or a moneymaking invention of the medieval Church, or a failure to believe that Christ truly redeemed us on Calvary, then the Catholic Church never did believe in such a thing. Nor should we uncritically accept the sometimes overly graphic and severe imagery that has been used to illustrate the doctrine of purgatory. The Ecumenical Councils of Lyons (1274), Florence (1439), and Trent (1545-63) forbade all fanciful elaborations, especially in public sermons. The *Catechism of the Catholic Church* chastely restricts its discussion of purgatory to only four paragraphs (see CCC, 1030-32, 1472).

"All who die in God's grace and friendship, but still imperfectly purified, are indeed assured of their eternal salvation; but after death they undergo purification, so as to achieve the holiness necessary to enter the joy of heaven" (CCC, 1030). Purgatory is that temporary state, place, condition, or process after death by which those who are in Christ are purged of disordered self-love and cleansed of remaining moral and spiritual imperfections.

Though most popular conversation and imagery presupposes purgatory as a "place," it is better to think about it in terms of "process." Our journey to heaven begins on earth. But if heaven is a place of mutual and unhampered love between God and human beings, then it appears that most of us end our earthly journey as flawed lovers, still inept at deep and sustained love. The purification begun on earth continues until we are rendered completely fit for eternal union with God.

Someone might object, "But aren't we forgiven in Christ? What remains to be done?" Forgiven, yes; transformed, not yet.[9] While God loves us the way we are right now, he loves us too much to let us stay that way. He accepts us where we are in order to move us to where he is.

We often die, however, with an unhealthy attachment to sin and still loving created things above our Creator. At the hour of our death our souls may not be fully fixed on evil, but neither are they fully fixed on the perfections of God. As Romano Guardini puts it, those who need further purification after death are those "whose intention has not penetrated sufficiently below the surface to reach the settled resistance beneath and the depths filled with evil and impurity,... whose whole life is riddled with omissions and bears in itself the ravages of wrongdoing."

We aren't unrepentant, just unperfected. The Spirit of Jesus dwells within us; the love of God has been shed abroad in our hearts (see Rom 5:5; 8:9). But we fall short of being the lovers who can embrace face-to-face communion with God, whose love is like a consuming fire (see Heb 12:29).

How are we to enter heaven, in which can dwell no unclean thing (see Rv 21:27)? How are we to dwell with a God whose eyes are too pure to behold iniquity (see Heb 4:13; Lv 11:44; 1 Pt 1:16)? How are we to enjoy fellowship with a God infinite in perfections when we lack perfection (see Mt 5:48)?

After all, heaven isn't filled with shy souls sporting "I'm Not Perfect, Just Forgiven" tee shirts. It's filled with glorious beings whose perfections move us like the sight of great mountains. Sadly, it appears that most of us die before that great transformation.

Some might ask, "Where is this grounded in Scripture?" For the ancient Hebrews, prayers for the dead were a pious act. "Withhold not kindness from the dead" (Sir 7:33). It is "a holy and pious thought" to pray for the dead (2 Mc 12:44-45; see also Ps 86:13; Acts 2:27).

Second-century Christian documents such as the *Acts of Paul and Thecla* and the *Martyrdom of Perpetua and Felicity* show us that the early Christians continued the practice. While these documents are not inspired Scripture, they indicate that prayers for the dead were not some outlandish later innovation, but rather an assumed and unquestioned practice.

The logic of this practice seems to demand purgatory. If the deceased are in heaven, they don't need our prayers. If they are in hell, our prayers won't do them any good. There must be a post-mortem place or condition that we can affect by our prayers.

Furthermore, Scripture describes a purifying fire some will pass through after death, which purges their souls of corrupt and combustible elements: "He himself will be saved, but only as through fire" (see 1 Cor 3:12-15).[10]

We must also consider what Jesus meant when he said that "whoever speaks against the Holy Spirit will not be forgiven, either in this age or in the age to come" (Mt 12:32). Certainly some possibility of post-death forgiveness is in view here.[11]

But wasn't the thief on the cross promised that on the day of his death, he would be with Christ in "paradise" (see Lk 23:43)? Yes. But what is "paradise"?

Christ descended into the realm of the dead and didn't return to heaven until his ascension, forty days after his resurrection (1 Pt 3:18-20; Eph 4:9-10). Further still, New Testament scholarship teaches that the term "paradise" in this passage doesn't refer to heaven.[12] It's a place of bliss and rest between death and resurrection. As to the conventional language of days, years, or centuries in purgatory, just remember that purgatory has no clock since it occurs outside of time.[13]

We might compare purgatory or the final purification, as I like to call it, to the antechamber of heaven. Imagine that you, a lame beggar, have received an invitation to the king's wedding supper. The invitation specifies that you arrive healthy, properly bathed, and in your best attire. The king's mansion is distant and can only be reached over perilous terrain. You fear you don't have the stamina, wardrobe, or courage to present yourself successfully at the supper.

Nevertheless, after all, the king has called you. So you set off for the banquet in this faraway land, growing in anticipation of intimate communion with the king and his guests. Along the way, your travel is full of travail. Yet it strengthens you. The rigorous exercise rids you of a respiratory condition you feared might disqualify you, and your atrophied leg begins to generate new muscle. The mud and briars, however, ruin your best clothes, and that old body odor that's clung to you for so long is still pungent enough to bring tears to the eyes of a musk ox.

When you arrive, the king's steward looks at the invitation and, pleased, says, "I can see you are in the king's good graces." He tries to usher you in for inspection before you are seated, but you demur. "Is there a place," you ask, "where I can shower and wash my clothes?"

The steward says, "Of course. We've provided all you need." He then lays out bathing oils and the robes you are to wear after your shower. Before you know it, you are indeed fit for a king.

Is purgatory then a place of suffering? Yes, but a suffering that refreshes. Suffering conforms us to Christ. "We are ... fellow heirs with Christ, provided we suffer with him in order that we may also be glorified with him" (Rom 8:16-17; 1 Pt 4:1; Heb 2:2-3). God squeezes us because he loves us. The psychotherapist Victor Frankl endured the horrors of a Nazi concentration camp. Drawing from that experience in his book *Man's Search for Meaning,* he insisted that we can endure any suffering as long as we believe it has a purpose. The soul in purgatory knows he is saved and destined for heaven.

As John Paul II has taught: "Life's earthly journey has an end which, if a person reaches it in friendship with God, coincides with the first moment of eternal bliss. Even, if in that passage to heaven, the soul must undergo the purification of the last impurities through purgatory, it is already filled with light, certitude, and joy, because the person knows that he belongs forever to God."[14]

This is not a new teaching. St. Catherine of Genoa (1447-1510) also believed that "no happiness can be found worthy to be compared with that of a soul in purgatory except that of the saints in Paradise. And day by day this happiness grows as God flows into these souls, more and more as the hindrance to his entrance is consumed. Sin's rust is the hindrance, and the fire burns the rust away so that more and more the soul opens itself up to the divine inflowing."[15]

Purgatory is not an extra-worldly concentration camp to punish us. Nor is it entirely the bliss of heaven. It better resembles a long awaited surgery that restores our health rather than a tornado that destroys our home.

V. Worship, Sacraments, and Sacramentals

Why seven sacraments?

The seven sacraments are baptism, penance, Eucharist, confirmation, matrimony, holy orders, and anointing of the sick.

The early Church did not precisely enumerate seven. St. Augustine, for example, in reply to a query, wrote: "[Christ] obliged the society of His new people to the Sacraments, very few in number, very easy of observance, and most sublime in meaning. Such, for example, is Baptism, consecrated in the name of the Trinity; the Communion of His Body and Blood; and whatever else is commended in the canonical Scriptures."[1] But he did not list the seven. In fact, burial, exorcisms, Lenten instructions, and even the profession of faith were, depending on the region, sometimes described under the rubric of "sacrament."

Occasionally, one will hear the charge that the Catholic Church didn't have seven sacraments until they were formally defined at the Council of Trent in the sixteenth century. This is false. Between 1100 and 1300 the sacraments were vigorously discussed in the schools and universities of Western Europe.

There was early agreement that the term "sacrament" should be used in the strict sense for only those seven rites that were instituted by Christ and give grace and divine life through the rite itself. Other prayers and actions, such as the sign of the cross or the conferral of ashes on Ash Wednesday, were useful for personal devotion and prayer for God's grace, but they were designated instead as "sacramentals."

But why seven sacraments? The simple answer is this: that's how many Christ instituted. But why did he institute seven? The Church has no definitive answer for this.

The Hebrew-Christian tradition is heavily invested with the symbolism of the number seven. Seven is the number of fullness. God instituted a seven-day week; Daniel prophesied that seventy weeks pinpointed the fullness of time for the appearance of the Messiah; Jesus told us to forgive seventy times seven; he spoke seven words from the cross; he sent out seventy disciples; and so on. How fitting that Christ's actions through his Church should bear the number seven symbolizing fullness of grace!

Some have also speculated that the seven sacraments mark and correspond to spiritual and developmental milestones or activities of the great human journey. Birth corresponds to baptism; eating and drinking, to the Eucharist; reconciliation, to penance; the passage into adulthood, to confirmation; commitment to solemn vows, to ordination and matrimony; illness and death, to the anointing of the sick. Through the sacraments, our lives are repeatedly punctuated by God's loving presence and strengthening grace at just the critical moments of our greatest need for him.

When all the explanation is said and done, however, only God knows with a certainty why there are seven sacraments, just as only he knows why we have two nostrils.

The fact that the Church didn't formally tally the seven at the beginning of the Christian era has led some critics to charge that the Church invented them later on. This fails to understand what we have earlier described as the "development of doctrine." The Church moves steadily from the Christ of the Gospels to the Christ in glory, and in doing so, the Church gradually became conscious of possessing seven sacraments.

Similarly, the Church used Scripture from its beginning, even though the first formal list of the books we call the "canon of Scripture" didn't appear until late into the fourth century. Nobody, however, accuses the Church of having invented the canon at that time. The essential thing is that she always possessed the sacraments as she did the Scriptures, and she lived in dependence on them as Christ's designated channels of grace.

In fact, certain Eastern Churches who began separating from the Catholic Church in the fifth century have themselves always maintained seven sacraments, as do the Eastern Orthodox, who separated in 1054. Their tradition testifies to the antiquity of the seven. Only at the Reformation was the total of seven denied, and as often happens, that crisis of dispute required the clarity of definition offered at the Council of Trent. Only many years after Christ's ascension, guided into all truth by the Spirit as promised by Jesus (Jn 15:26; 16:14), did the Church fully articulate the number and nature of the seven sacraments.

An analogy might be helpful here. The shepherds got to Bethlehem and found Mary and Joseph and the infant Jesus lying in the manger. Enthusiasm flowed as they told about the angels they had seen and what they had revealed about the child. But what could they have told Mary that she didn't already know? Apparently, enough that "Mary kept all these things, pondering them in her heart" (Lk 2:19).

Think of it. Although Mary had herself received an angelic revelation about Jesus (Lk 1:26-38); and had heard Elizabeth exclaim, "And why is this granted me, that the mother of my Lord should come to me?" (Lk 1:43); and was told that Elizabeth's unborn child John leaped in the womb as the unborn Jesus approached (Lk 1:44); and had carried the gestating Jesus in her womb for nine months; yet she still had to ponder and chew upon the significance of these events. Their meaning wasn't transparently clear. There was still more light to break forth from God's word.

The Church is like Mary in this respect. She, as a mother, is impregnated with the Divine Word and transmits this Word to the world. Yet like Mary, though she has received divine revelation, she must in time continue to ponder and unfold the revelation she has received.

Do Catholics really believe the Eucharist is literally the Body and Blood of Christ?

Yes!—although, like Thomas Aquinas, sometimes called the "Eucharistic Doctor," we recognize that the Eucharist is a mystery that no theological explanation can hope to exhaust fully. The physico-chemical mechanisms involved will probably always remain a mystery.

Jesus' words are simple and clear: "Now as they were eating, Jesus took bread, and blessed, and broke it, and gave it to the disciples and said, 'Take, eat; this is my body.' And he took a cup, and when he had given thanks he gave it to them, saying, 'Drink of it, all of you; for this is my blood of the covenant, which is poured out for many for the forgiveness of sins'" (Mt 26:26-28; see also Mk 14:22-25; Lk 22:19-20; 1 Cor 11:24-25).

During the gathering of Protestant leaders in 1529 called the Marburg Colloquy, even Martin Luther, still clarifying his own thought, almost came to blows over this issue with Ulrich Zwingli, another prominent Protestant reformer. "This *is* my body!" Luther reportedly shouted over Zwingli's protests, because the latter had denied Christ's real presence in the rite.

Catholics believe that when the bread and wine are consecrated by a priest, united with Christ through a valid ordination and intending to so consecrate, a change takes place in their substance. They become the Body and Blood of our Lord and Savior Jesus Christ. This change is technically called "transubstantiation." When Catholics receive the Eucharist they are truly receiving Jesus' Body, Blood, Soul and Divinity.

Many find this difficult to believe. But the same God who created all things out of nothing, I like to think, probably finds it a little easier actually to create something out of bread and wine. At least he's got something to start with. Remember: Christ's words are potent. Through him, who is the Word, the divine Logos, all things came into existence (see Jn 1:1-3; Col 1:15-17).

St. John Chrysostom (c. 344-407) understood this when he preached: "For it is not man who makes the sacrificial gifts become the Body and Blood of Christ, but he that was crucified for us, Christ himself. The priest stands there carrying out the action, but the power and the grace is of God. 'This is my Body,' he says. This statement transforms the gifts."[2]

St. Ambrose (c. 333-97) also makes this point wonderfully after referring to the miracles performed through the ministries of Moses and Elijah:

But if the Word of Elijah had such power as to bring down fire from heaven, shall not the word of Christ have power to change the nature of the elements? You read concerning the making of the whole world: 'He spake and they were made, He commanded and they were created.' Shall not the word of Christ, which was able to make out of nothing that which was not, be able to change things which already are into what they were not? For it is not less to give a new nature to things than to change them."[3]

How do we know that in the consecrated bread and wine we really have Christ? We know it by revelation—the same way we know that Christ is God. He is a divine Person who appeared as a human being. The divine manifests himself under the appearance of the earthly.

If we had performed an autopsy on Jesus the moment he was taken down from the cross, we would not have had any physical evidence that he was God. His pituitary gland wouldn't be engraved with an inscription, "I am that I am." His heart would not have an eternal flame burning inside it. His lungs wouldn't be stamped: "Courtesy of the breath of God."

So how do we know he is God? By divine revelation. "Blessed are you, Simon Bar Jona," Jesus said to Peter. "For flesh and blood has not revealed this to you, but my Father who is in heaven" (Mt 16:17). We know Christ under the appearance of bread and wine as well as through divine revelation, so I will focus primarily on a few Scripture texts.

By the time the Gospel of John was written, the Christian communities had been practicing the Lord's Supper for nearly sixty years. The Eucharistic significance of the following discourse wouldn't have escaped them:

> "I am the bread of life. Your fathers ate the manna in the wilderness, and they died.... I am the living bread which came down from heaven; if any one eats of this bread, he will live forever; and the bread which I shall give for the life of the world is my flesh." The Jews then disputed among themselves, saying: "How can this man give us his flesh to eat?" So Jesus said to them: "Truly, truly, I say to you, unless you eat the flesh of the Son of man and drink his blood, you have no life in you; he who eats my flesh and drinks my blood has eternal life, and I will raise him up at the last day. For my flesh is food indeed, and my blood is drink indeed.... This is the bread which came down from heaven, not such as the fathers ate and died; he who eats this bread will live for ever."
>
> JOHN 6:48-49, 51-55, 58

In the Eucharist, Jesus offers us something superior even to the supernatural heavenly food by which God nourished the children of Israel. If the Eucharist is merely symbolic earthly bread and wine, however, wouldn't it really be inferior to the manna?

I suppose the best interpreters of Jesus' words are those who were listening to him. What was their reaction? They took his words literally; some were scandalized and abandoned him.

"How can this man give us his flesh to eat?" they insisted (Jn 6:52). "This is a hard saying; who can listen to it?" (v. 60). If they had interpreted his words in a figurative sense, it would not have been a hard saying. There would have been no offense.

But Jesus, the Lover of our souls and the Master Communicator, did nothing to call them back. He didn't try to correct any misconceptions they might have been laboring under, as he had previously done in a conversation with Rabbi Nicodemus (see Jn 3:1-15). He spoke forcefully and with a double Amen—that is, "Truly, truly." To sharpen the point, Jesus employed a verb that means "to munch or gnaw" and not simply to ingest.

How did the early Church understand the Eucharist? St. Paul writes:

> The cup of blessing which we bless, is it not a participation in the blood of Christ? The bread which we break, is it not a participation in the body of Christ? ... Whoever, therefore, eats the bread or drinks the cup of the Lord in an unworthy manner will be guilty of profaning the body and blood of the Lord. Let a man examine himself, and so eat of the bread and drink of the cup. For any one who eats and drinks without discerning the body eats and drinks judgment upon himself. That is why many of you are weak and ill, and some have died.
>
> 1 CORINTHIANS 10:16; 11:27-30

In the bread and wine, the early Church believed it received and shared in the actual, not merely the symbolic, Body and Blood of Christ. This is no mere ceremonial food. A gravity and an aura surround this table that is not shared by other communal meals.

We're commanded to inspect ourselves in two ways before we participate. First, we must examine ourselves, because spiritual fitness is a precondition to receiving the Eucharistic Savior. Second, we must recognize the Body of the Lord in the ritual.

This recollection is done with good reason! The one who partakes unworthily will have to answer for the Body and Blood of the Lord. But what is there to answer for if in the Eucharist we're only dealing with a loaf of bread and a carafe of wine?

If a vandal destroyed a famous painting of George Washington, we wouldn't tell him that he is guilty of profaning the body and the blood of the George. Why would one have to answer for unworthily receiving the Body and Blood of the Lord, if all he was ingesting was bread and wine?

Jesus' holy presence is so identified with the Eucharist that to commune with him unworthily might provoke a severe trauma of physical judgment and even death. This is one reason Catholics are not to partake of the Body and Blood if they are burdened with the guilt of mortal sin. It's as though the altar were a large potbelly stove that's radiating a fiery love to all who approach it. But if you don't respect it—if you dance carelessly around it—you'll get burned.

In about the year 258, St. Cyprian of Carthage mentioned stories that testify to this ongoing danger of receiving unworthily. "This one," he noted, "attempting to communicate amongst the faithful, is seized by horrible convulsions. That one, striving to open the tabernacle in which the Body of the Lord was preserved, sees flames issuing forth."

What did the early Church think, since they were closest to the

Incarnation? The fathers of the Church echo the language of the New Testament. Sixty-three teachers flourishing from the first through the sixth centuries all proclaimed the Real Presence. Take, for example, a letter of St. Ignatius, bishop of Antioch, written about the year 100— a time, most scholars agree, just after the last of the apostles had died. Speaking of certain heretics, he said: "They abstain from the Eucharist and prayer, because they refuse to confess that the Eucharist is the flesh of our Savior, Jesus Christ."[4]

What are the parts of the Mass?

In its most basic structure, the Mass is like a nut. Skillfully cracked, it splits into two balanced halves: the Liturgy of the Word and the Liturgy of the Eucharist. Using a different analogy to explain this division, St. Augustine wrote of two tables: "From the table of the Lord we receive our food, bread of life,... and from the table of Sunday readings we are nourished with the doctrine of the Lord."

The Mass is thus like an extraordinary banquet that is best appreciated as you read the menu ahead of time and anticipate the flow of the courses. We begin this spiritual banquet by clearing our palette through sipping the Introductory Rites.

In the *Introductory Rites* we prepare to meet God. The *Entrance Song (Introit)* sets the tone as the priest and the other ministers of the Mass process toward the altar. We, a pilgrim people journeying toward eternity, rejoice! (Ps 43:3-4).

The *Greeting* occurs after the priest has reverenced the altar with a kiss. He makes the sign of the cross, reminding us of our baptism in the name of the Trinity, and greets us in words of Scripture: "The Lord be with you." The assembly heartily responds: "And also with you."[5]

The *Penitential Rite* follows; it solemnly slows the pace inviting us to repent before we enter the sacred mysteries. "I confess to Almighty God and to you, my brothers and sisters ..." After this general confession (the *Confiteor*) we plead for God's mercy in the *Kyrie*: "Lord have mercy, Christ have mercy, Lord have mercy."[6] The priest, in the person of Christ, responds with a prayer of absolution, reconciling us with God and reminding us of our true identity: sons and daughters of a loving God.[7] We forgiven sinners now sing the *Gloria* and cross the threshold into God's merciful presence and set about rejoicing again.[8]

The *Opening Prayer* used to be called the *Collect* because the priest invites us to "collect" our prayers during a moment of silence. He then offers a prayer that becomes the tuning fork of the Mass. From this prayer we get the pitch of the worship for the day. We approve the prayer offered in our name with an "Amen"—that is, "So be it."[9] Like the *Entrance Song* and, later, the readings, the *Opening Prayer* varies according to the Mass of the day.

With the *Opening Prayer* the *Introductory Rites* come to an end, and we are prepared to enter into the heart of the Mass.

In the *Liturgy of the Word*, God speaks to us. Only Scripture is read, and we find ourselves exhorted, rebuked, consoled, encouraged, challenged, and instructed.[10]

The scriptural readings are arranged in a three-year cycle contained in a liturgical book called the *Lectionary*. If a Catholic attended only Sunday Mass over the three-year period, he would hear over seven thousand verses that include nearly the entire New Testament and all significant portions of the Old Testament. If he attended daily Mass, he would hear over fourteen thousand verses in just a two-year period.

The *first reading* is usually taken from the Old Testament or Acts, is keyed to the Gospel reading, and demonstrates how the Hebrew Bible prepared for the coming of the full revelation of God in the Incarnation.

A *Psalm response* is then either recited or sung by the assembly, meditating on the reading and eliciting emotions of joy, perplexity, fear, melancholy, despair, trust, or anger.

The *second reading* is usually taken from the epistles or the Book of Revelation.

The *Gospel* has pride of place among the readings. It is preceded by an Alleluia and "Glory to you, Lord" and climaxed by "Praise to you, Lord Jesus Christ."

The *homily* must be preached by someone ordained and applies the Word to everyday life and the liturgical year.

After some meditative silence, we acclaim the whole story of redemption from creation to final judgment in the *Profession of Faith (the Creed).* As Fr. Peter Stravinskas has put it: "The Creed was inserted into the liturgy as a means of ensuring that only true believers would remain for the Liturgy of the Eucharist."[11] We are now moving toward the deepest mystery: the Incarnation. If one cannot say the Creed with confidence, he is not ready to enter into full communion with Christ, who will soon be present in his Body, Blood, Soul, and Divinity.

The *General Intercessions (Prayers of the Faithful)* further unite us with our great High Priest, who always makes intercession on our behalf (Heb 7:25). After the priest opens the prayer, a lector reads the specific prayer intentions and the people respond by asking, "Lord, hear our prayer." With a prayer, the priest concludes the *Liturgy of the Word,* and we are ready for the greatest mystery, the *Liturgy of the Eucharist,* the Word made flesh.

In the *Liturgy of the Eucharist,* God comes to us. Just as the *Liturgy of the Word* was preceded by a period of preparation, so too is the *Liturgy of the Eucharist.*

In the *preparation of the altar and the gifts,* the chalice is prepared at the altar as the assembly sings a hymn related to the liturgical season and the ushers take up the sacrificial collection. From earliest times God's covenant people have offered the first fruits of the work of their hands.[12] As the Jewish theologian Abraham Herschel once said: "All that we own, we owe."

In the *presentation of and prayer over the gifts (the Offertory)*, members of the assembly carry the unleavened bread and the wine to the altar. The priest prays that these gifts of the earth and the work of human hands would become "for us the bread of life" and "our spiritual drink." The assembly prays that "our sacrifice may be acceptable to God, the Almighty Father."[13]

The *Eucharistic Prayer* begins with a dialogue: "The Lord be with you," the priest says. The people wish him equally well: "And also with you."

The *Preface*, the *Sanctus*, and the *Benedictus* then start as a poem of praise and thanksgiving for God's work in creation and redemption. They end, however, by echoing the angels and all the company of heaven, who join us in acclaiming Isaiah's awesome vision of God in the temple: "Holy, Holy, Holy" (Is 6:3; Ps 19:2; 118:26; Mt 21:9). The Lord is drawing near: "Blessed is he who comes in the name of the Lord" (Mt 21:9). Anticipation of his coming builds.

Next, the Holy Spirit is invoked (the *Epiclesis*) to transform the gifts into the Body and Blood of Christ.

Christ's *Words of Institution* (the *Consecration*), from the Gospels and St. Paul, immediately follow. Although the entire Eucharistic prayer is consecratory, the bread and wine are traditionally understood to be transformed at this time.[14]

The priest intones: "Let us proclaim the mystery of faith" (see 1 Tm 3:16), to which the people offer one of several *Memorial Acclamations*, such as "Christ has died, Christ is risen, Christ will come again." Then follows prayers for the Church and its leaders.

The priest acknowledges this mystery that is now born in our midst by saying: "Through him, with him, in him, in the unity of the Holy Spirit all glory and honor is yours, almighty God and Father forever and ever." And the people respond in a "Great Amen" (Rom 16:27; Gal 1:5; 1 Tm 1:17; Jude 25). The Eucharistic prayer is over.

Next comes the *Communion Rite.* Since the Mass is simultaneously the memorial of the death and resurrection of Christ, a sacrifice in which the cross is revealed, and a sacred family banquet in which we anticipate sharing the Wedding Supper of the Lamb, great emphasis is put on sharing this together.[15]

We begin with the *Lord's Prayer* (or the *Our Father*). The "O" in "Our" needs to be wide enough to include God's children from all nations, kindred, and tongues, because this unity is a sign of the kingdom (see Mt 6:13-14; Lk 6:38; Rv 7:11-12).

The *Sign of Peace* follows our prayer for the coming of the kingdom and our willingness to forgive the trespasses of others. Here we rehearse our acceptance of all those who, whether we like it or not, will be in heaven, and we demonstrate some appropriate gesture of reconciliation with our brothers and sisters, the lovely as well as the unlovely, the boor as well as the charming.[16]

In the *breaking of the bread* and "*Lamb of God*" (*Agnus Dei*) we pray: "Lamb of God, who takes away the sin of the world, have mercy on us." In response to our plea, the priest breaks the sacred Host, holds it up before the assembly, and declares: "This is the Lamb of God who takes away the sins of the world. Happy are those who are called to his supper." With the centurion, we respond: "Lord, I am not worthy to receive you, but only say the word and I shall be healed."[17]

The *Communion* now begins with song as the people file forward to receive the Body, Blood, Soul, and Divinity of Christ, a community reconciled to God and to each other.

When offering the sacred Species, the minister says, "The Body of Christ," to which the communicant must answer, "Amen"—that is, "So be it." If one doesn't so believe, he should refrain from partaking for reasons of conscience (Ex 16:4; Jn 6:60-65; 1 Cor 11:27-29).

The *prayer after Communion* and the cleansing of the sacred vessels concludes the Communion Rite and the Liturgy of the Eucharist.

In the *Concluding Rite,* we go forth as God's ambassadors. God's people have gathered, and he has come into their midst. We are sent off into the world with the familiar words that through the liturgy have been made far weightier: "The Lord be with you." We respond, "And also with you." The priest then confers a blessing on the people, to which they reply, "Amen."

What follows is as significant as anything that has gone on in the sacred assembly. A transformed people is dismissed to reenter the world of space and time so they can transform it into the kingdom of God. The priest tells us, "Go in peace to love and serve the Lord," and we respond, "Thanks be to God" (Gn 12:1-3; Ex 25:8; Ps 1:1-2; 150:6).

Why do Catholics confess to a priest?

Catholics confess to a priest because they first went to Jesus, and he told them to go to a priest. Christ himself determined to forgive and retain sins through human intermediaries.

After his resurrection, Jesus appeared to his disciples and said: "'Peace be with you. As the Father has sent me, even so I send you.' And when he had said this, he breathed on them, and said to them, 'Receive the Holy Spirit. If you forgive the sins of any, they are forgiven; if you retain the sins of any, they are retained'" (Jn 20:21-23).

The apostles and their successors don't merely proclaim forgiveness to those who repent; they can also "retain"—that is, refuse to confer absolution for sins. They have the discretionary power of "binding and loosing." Jesus commissioned his community on earth to speak in his name not just metaphorically, but metaphysically. The sacrament of penance as a mediation of Christ's work is dictated by the logic of the Incarnation.

Catholics believe that Jesus is, quite literally, present on the earth today carrying out his ministry of the forgiveness of sins through the body, the Church, that acts in and bears his name. God was present to us in the flesh two thousand years ago; he continues to impart his grace in a fully personal way through those, beginning with the apostles, whom he has ordained to perpetuate his mission from the Father.

How are that grace and forgiveness mediated, that is, made visible and manifest, to us? Pope John Paul notes: "God is always the one who is principally offended by sin—'I have sinned against You'—and God alone can forgive." He does so through the ministry of the priest in the sacrament of penance, "the only ordinary way in which the faithful who are conscious of serious sin are reconciled with God and with the Church."[18]

The sacrament of penance is the "ordinary" way of reconciliation. But God is not limited to the sacrament of penance. We all rejoice in stories of people who are released from oppressive sin and guilt through the mediation of an evangelist or preacher, but who haven't a clue about this sacrament. Yet God has explicitly instructed us that he normally forgives sins through the instrumentality of human priests who are ordained to visibly represent Christ's unique priesthood.

We must hold together two biblical truths: First, only God can forgive sins. Second, he does so through human agents.

Consider this Gospel account:

And when [Jesus] returned to Capernaum after some days, it was reported that he was at home. And many were gathered together, so that there was no longer room for them, not even about the door; and he was preaching the word to them. And they came, bringing to him a paralytic carried by four men. And when they could not get near him because of the crowd, they removed the roof above him; and when they had made an opening, they let down the pallet on which the paralytic lay. And when Jesus saw their faith, he said to the paralytic, "My son, your sins are forgiven." Now some of the scribes were sitting there, questioning in their hearts, "Why does this man speak thus? It is blasphemy! Who can forgive sins but God alone?"

MARK 2:1-7

Huh? What do the scribes mean that only God can forgive sin?

I'm still married because my wife regularly forgives sins. Aren't we all called to forgive one another? When my brother Michael and I stupidly argued a few years ago, he forgave me for the harsh words I spoke. But I didn't take his generous spirit as evidence of his divinity.

Imagine, though, if we had come to blows, and as I was lifting myself off the floor, our neighbor Jack sauntered by, stood between us, turned to me, and said, "Don't worry, Al. I forgive Michael." I would be outraged. "Wait a minute, Jack! Michael hasn't sinned against *you*. He's sinned against *me*. By what authority do you forgive him this sin?"

Now back to our story: When had the paralytic sinned against Jesus of Nazareth? He hadn't. What were the sins Jesus was forgiving? It could only be sins committed against either other men or God himself. Unless he is himself the God who is the offended party in all sins, this would be an act of colossal arrogance.

Yet this is what Jesus did. As C.S. Lewis has written:

He told people that their sins were forgiven and never waited to consult all the other people whom their sins had undoubtedly injured. He unhesitatingly behaved as if he was the party chiefly concerned, the person chiefly offended in all offenses. This makes sense only if he really was the God whose laws are broken, whose love is wounded in every sin. In the mouth of any speaker who is not God, these words would imply what can only be regarded as a silliness and conceit unrivalled by any other character in history.[19]

But if only God can ultimately forgive sins, why a priest? In Hebrew and the later Christian tradition, confession of sin was never just a private matter between me and God or me and Jesus. God's people have always commissioned particular individuals from among the people to speak forgiveness on behalf of God as well as the community.

For the ancient Israelite, confession of sin was much more complicated than for us. People offered up sin sacrifices and trespass offerings involving cattle, goats, or sheep and requiring the ministry of the priest and the altar. The confessor would raise a knife to cut, rip, and separate the parts of the sacrifice as he sang songs of repentance and praise. The priest simply handled all the ritual parts that related directly to the altar.

Confession of sin was personal, public, messy, and costly. When the people of God in the Old Covenant went to God for the forgiveness of sin, what did God say? "Bring your sin offering to the priest" (see Heb 5:1; Mal 2:7 on the role of the priest).

The New Covenant doesn't abolish but rather fulfills the Old, and now Jesus is our High Priest (see Heb 7:1-10, 15-17; Col 1:19-20). While the Old laid down the pattern for the people of God, the New fulfills that pattern in a more glorious, effective, and satisfying form. Christ transformed the sacrificial system. His death put an end to the bloody sacrifice of lambs and goats. He is now our sin offering, "the Lamb of God, who takes away the sins of the world" (see Jn 1:29).

The *Catechism* describes it this way:

In imparting to his apostles his own power to forgive sins the Lord also gives them the authority to reconcile sinners with the Church.... "I will give you the keys of the kingdom of heaven, and whatever you bind on earth shall be bound in heaven, and whatever you loose on earth shall be loosed in heaven."[20] ... Since Christ entrusted to his apostles the ministry of reconciliation,[21] bishops who are their successors, and priests, the bishops' collaborators, continue to exercise this ministry. Indeed bishops and priests, by virtue of the sacrament of Holy Orders, have the power to forgive all sins "in the name of the Father, and of the Son, and of the Holy Spirit" (CCC, 1444, 1461).

Given the greatness of this ministry, priests are sworn to absolute secrecy. No government or church leader has authority to demand knowledge of a sacramental confession. The priest can make no use of the knowledge he acquires in the confessional. The Alfred Hitchcock thriller *I Confess* in fact bases its suspenseful plot on this prohibition (see CCC, 1467).

Throughout Scripture, humans mediate God's love, healing, forgiveness, and instruction.

Is any one among you sick? Let him call for the elders of the church, and let them pray over him, anointing him with oil in the name of the Lord; and the prayer of faith will save the sick man, and the Lord will raise him up; and if he has committed sins, he will be forgiven. Therefore confess your sins to one another, and pray for one another, that you may be healed. The prayer of a righteous man has great power in its effects.

JAMES 5:14-16

See also 1 CORINTHIANS 5:1-13

Here again the confession of sin is no merely private matter, but rather takes place in the context of summoning the elders of the church.

So Catholics ultimately confess to God, who alone can forgive sins. The priest, for his part, visibly extends Christ's priestly ministry, the same way the preacher extends Christ's prophetic ministry. In creation, God fashioned human beings in his image and likeness to carry out his reign and rule over the earth. In redemption, he once again resorts to the human agents he has created in his image (see Gn 1:26-28; Ps 8:5-8; Eph 4:24; Col 3:10; Heb 2:5-9; Jas 3:9).

When we confess to a priest we are confessing to Christ, the one High Priest who carries out his ministry through the ordained priesthood.

Aren't all Christians priests?

Yes and no.

Yes, all those who by faith and baptism are united to Christ share in his role as prophet, priest, and king. Addressing an audience of both clergy and laity, St. Peter urged: "Like living stones be yourselves built into a spiritual house, to be a holy priesthood, to offer spiritual sacrifices acceptable to God through Jesus Christ.... You are a chosen race, a royal priesthood, a holy nation, God's own people" (1 Pt 2:5, 9; see also Rv 1:6; 5:10; 20:6).

But no, we aren't all ordained to the ministerial priesthood. Jesus' command to the Twelve to "do this in remembrance of me" presupposes an ongoing ministerial priesthood to perform this ritual action until he comes again in glory. There is absolutely no evidence from the Scripture or Sacred Tradition that just any Christian could perform the ritual action we call the Eucharist.[22]

While the New Testament contains many terms for Church office, including deacons, presbyters, pastors, bishops, apostles, prophets, teachers, and so on, the threefold division of bishop, presbyter (priest), and deacon was recognized early on.[23] From the beginning of the Church, the Eucharist was celebrated by the bishops, who were the successors of the apostles, and then—as the Church grew in numbers—by his delegates, the presbyters (priests).

Some denominations teach that under the Old Covenant we needed a ministerial priesthood, but since the coming of Christ, we are all priests. But this fails to understand the proper balance between continuity and discontinuity between the covenants.

Ancient Israel, like the Church, the "Israel of God" (Gal 6:16), had a universal as well as a ministerial priesthood. Long before the Church was called "a kingdom of priests, a holy nation" (1 Pt 2:9; Rev 5:10), the people of ancient Israel were called a "kingdom of priests" (Ex 19:6). But even though all the Israelite people were priests, the nation also had, by divine ordination, a ministerial priesthood drawn from the universal priesthood of the people and set apart for ritual and cultic service at the altar (see Ex 19:22; 28:1).

What's new about the New Covenant priesthood is that Christ is the unique Priest according to the order of Melchizedek rather than that of Aaron or Levi (see Gn 14:18-20; Ps 110:4; Heb 5-7; 8:5; Col 2:17). His priesthood is a matter of union with God, not biological ancestry. All those who are ordained in his name operate *in persona Christi capitis,* that is, in the Person of Christ, the Head.

Most people don't realize that the Catholic Church teaches that under the New Covenant, there is only one Priest, just as there is only one King, one Prophet, one Mediator, and one Shepherd.[24] But Christ's priesthood is given visible expression and effectiveness in space and time through those ordained as his priests. Their priesthood is Christ's, and they possess no priesthood apart from that of Christ. It is his priesthood to which they are united and which they pledge to extend into the world.[25]

The ministerial priesthood celebrates the sacraments, proclaims the prophetic word, and governs and shepherds Christ's people in his name. While all Christians share in Christ's work as prophet, priest, and king, the ordained priest shares this work with Christ in a mode and office different from that of the lay faithful.

This distinction between a universal call and a particular office is common in biblical thought. For instance, the Greek word for "sent one or envoy" is *apostolos,* from which we get "apostle." Jesus is the "Sent One" whom the Father consecrated and sent into the world (see Jn 10:36; Heb 3:1).

All Christians are likewise consecrated through baptism and sent into the world as envoys and ambassadors of the kingdom (2 Cor 5:20). You might say that we have a universal apostleship just as we have a universal priesthood. Nevertheless, we recognize a special office of "sent one," that is, "apostle."[26] In the same way, all Christians are "ministers" or "servants," but not all hold the office of *diakonos*—that is, "deacon," which literally means "minister" or "servant."[27]

Sometimes people say that the ministerial priesthood obscures Christ's unique priesthood. But this is no more true than the claim that the existence of prophets or teachers or pastors and shepherds within the Church obscures Christ's unique role as the Prophet, Teacher, or Shepherd, or that the existence of apostles—that is, "sent ones"—detracts from Christ as the unique "Sent One" from the Father. Neither the ministerial priesthood nor the universal priesthood should render doubtful or ambiguous Christ's unique priesthood.

In fact, the universal priesthood of the laity is designed to transform the world, while the ministerial priesthood exists to serve the laity in that calling to renew the face of the earth. The Second Vatican Council declared:

> For all their works, prayers, and apostolic undertakings, family and married life, daily work, relaxation of mind and body, if they are accomplished in the Spirit—indeed even the hardships of life if patiently borne—all these become spiritual sacrifices acceptable to God through Jesus Christ (see 1 Pt 2:5). In the celebration of the Eucharist, these may most fittingly be offered to the Father along with the body of the Lord.... The laity consecrates the world itself to God.[28]

Why are Catholic priests celibate?

Surprise! Some are and some aren't. The Eastern rite Catholic Churches regularly ordain married men. This has been their custom from very early times. The Western Latin rite Church has generally preferred celibacy and eventually made it the norm. But even the Latin rite occasionally ordains married men if they have been Protestant clergy and have then sought ordination after entering the Catholic Church.

Here an important point should be made. Catholics distinguish between the changing disciplines of the Church and the immutable Sacred Tradition, the "deposit of faith" the Church has been charged to guard. Sacred Tradition preserves doctrines first taught by Jesus to the apostles and later passed down to us through the apostles' successors, the bishops. Customs and disciplines, on the other hand, adapt divine law to help us carry out and apply Sacred Tradition.

For instance, Jesus commanded us to pray. That is doctrine. The rosary, however, is simply one specific way of praying. It is a discipline. Jesus taught us to fast. Not eating meat on Fridays in Lent is an application of his doctrine.

Jesus and St. Paul taught that the gift of celibacy empowered certain gifted people to serve others better. Priestly celibacy is an application of this teaching. There is no universal and immutable command that priests must forever be celibate. So all priests may one day marry if the Church comes to believe that such a change better serves its pastoral mission.

Anti-Catholics often mistakenly believe that the Catholic Church teaches that priestly celibacy is an irreformable dogma. Then they delight in pointing out that St. Peter and many early bishops appear to have been married (see 1 Cor 9:5; 1 Tm 3:2-4). Yes, for centuries, priests were allowed to marry, just as they are today in the Eastern rites. No Catholic denies this, although some new scholarly works have recently been published arguing for the apostolic origins of priestly celibacy.

What the critics fail to understand is this difference between what is a discipline of the Church and what is Sacred Tradition. Sometimes they go further out on a limb and charge that the Catholic Church is teaching a "doctrine of demons" (1 Tm 4:1-3) by forbidding marriage.

They seem to forget that marriage is celebrated and encouraged as a sacrament in the Catholic Church.

Catholics happen to believe that Jesus created sex; it was his idea. Yet he chose to remain celibate. Regarding priests, no one is forbidding even them to marry, since no one is required to become a priest.

So why extend the Lord's and St. Paul's general teaching on celibacy specifically to the ministerial priesthood? Paul gave us a very practical reason: an unmarried man is freer to serve Christ and his Church (1 Cor 7:7-8, 28, 32-35).

For instance, imagine a married priest with a teenage daughter. She has a violin recital the same night that the parish high school basketball team is competing in the state championship. What event should he attend? Who better needs his symbolic and moral support? He is divided.

The unmarried priest doesn't have to make such a choice. He is given over entirely to the Church. He can function as a father to his parish without fear of neglecting his own flesh and blood.

Some wonder whether an unmarried priest can really sympathize with marriage and family tensions the way a married priest can. But aren't priests also sons of a mother? Didn't they grow up in families with brothers and sisters and cousins with all the accompanying conflicts and consanguinities? The priest hasn't dropped into this world from some relationally antiseptic corner of the cosmos.

We don't expect psychiatrists to have suffered a bout of mental illness in order to treat depressed clients. Art critics don't have to be painters to comment thoughtfully on Fra Angelico, Van Gogh, or Jackson Pollack. Criminal attorneys don't have to be murder defendants before they can successfully defend one.

A second reason for a celibate priesthood is to guarantee that even in this world some within the Church will be living witnesses to our future state of life in heaven. "For in the resurrection they neither marry nor are given in marriage, but are like angels in heaven" (Mt 22:30). So by choosing to be celibates, priests serve as a sign of the resurrection life to come and also render plausible for others the present possibility of chaste behavior in this sex-saturated society.

This witness is, perhaps, more important than ever before in Western history. Our culture harbors an almost mystical notion that sex is the spice of life and everything can be better seasoned with it. Advertising, music, theatre, humor, all conspire to create the impression that sex equals maturity, and lack of sex means immaturity. By maintaining a largely celibate priesthood, the Catholic Church always keeps before our eyes living examples of those who are so sharply oriented to the coming kingdom that they joyfully deny themselves some of this world's goods, such as marriage and offspring.

There is, however, a deeper theological reason for preferring an unmarried priesthood. The priest finds his identity in being a continuation of Christ himself. While this is true for all Christians generally, it is especially so for those who are ordained to the ministerial priesthood. Baptism imprints the pattern of Christ's death and resurrection on the soul of all Christians (see Rom 6:3-4). Ordination, however, lays down another, even deeper, template of conformity to Christ.

The priest is ordained to act in the person of Christ and to serve the Church in a distinct way. He "acts out" Jesus' priesthood through the sacrifice of the Mass, which sacramentally represents Christ's atoning death on Calvary. We hear the priest standing in the place of Christ and intoning his words, "This is my Body.... This is my Blood." He tangibly extends Jesus' forgiveness by pronouncing the words of absolution in the sacrament of penance.

In all these ways, the priest functions as an icon of Christ. Celibacy is but a further resemblance to Jesus' manner of life.

Even further, the Church is the Bride of Christ. The priest seeks to live out and make visible Christ's husbandly love for his Bride, the Church. Pope John Paul II observes this mystery of Christ and the Church: "[Ordination] configures the priest to Jesus Christ, the Head and Spouse of the Church. The Church as the Spouse of Jesus Christ wishes to be loved by the priest in the total and exclusive manner in which Jesus Christ her Head and Spouse loves her. Priestly celibacy, then, is the gift of self in and with Christ to his Church and expresses the priest's service to the Church and in the Lord."[29]

The priest is called to be the living image of Jesus Christ, the Spouse of the Church. He is called to live out Christ's spousal love towards the Church. The priest is therefore not without spousal love; he has as his bride the Church. So in a very real way, we shouldn't think of the celibate priest as unmarried. He is married, as Jesus is, to the Church. His celibacy reminds us of this reality.

Those who belittle celibacy simply don't know celibacy as St. Augustine, St. Thomas Aquinas, or Mother Theresa knew celibacy. Celibacy is a divine calling heard, not a romantic whisper ignored; a heroic choice exercised, not a natural urge repressed; a gift unwrapped, not a tax extracted. The Holy Spirit for reasons of his own bestows on certain people this gift so they can more ardently pursue the kingdom of God and serve God's people.

When the celibate recognizes the gift and begins to act on it, he discovers that his love is not limited to one, but mysteriously and joyfully spreads to all. Celibacy is not the repression of erotic love, but the radiation of divine love.

Why do Catholics violate Jesus' teaching by calling priests "Father"?

In Matthew chapter 23, Jesus warns against the behavior of the scribes and Pharisees who exalt themselves and covet the seats of honor at public banquets and synagogues. They use their religious authority to bask in the praise of people while at the same time making void the Word of God and oppressing the common believer.

Jesus says to his followers: "But you are not to be called rabbi, for you have one teacher, and you are all brethren. And call no man your father on earth, for you have one Father, who is in heaven. Neither be called masters, for you have one master, the Christ. He who is greatest among you shall be your servant; whoever exalts himself will be humbled, and whoever humbles himself will be exalted" (Mt 23:8-12).

In light of this passage, some Christians believe that the Catholic, Eastern Orthodox, and Episcopalian custom of calling their priests "Father" ignores Jesus' clear words. But this interpretation of the passage ends up proving too much. If it forbids any honorific title, then what are we to make of common Protestant titles such as pastor, reverend, teacher, doctor, and bishop?

When taken with wooden literalness, the passage even forbids calling our biological or adoptive male parent "father"—after all, we're to call *no* one on earth "father," because our real "Father" is in heaven. And what should we call our family physician, since "Doctor" is taken from the Latin word for "teacher"? Should we cease using the title of "Mister," which is derived from "master"?

Far more seriously, this strictly literal application of the passage mocks the practice of the very apostles we are called to emulate. The New Testament writers affectionately called Jewish or Christian leaders "father." Consider St. Paul, for example:

- He called Abraham "the father of all who believe,... our father" (Rom 4:11-12; see also Acts 7:2).
- He also referred to himself this way: "like a father with his children, we exhorted each one of you" (1 Thes 2:11).
- He told the Corinthians: "For though you have countless guides in Christ, you do not have many fathers. For I became your father in Christ Jesus through the gospel. I urge you, then, be imitators of me" (1 Cor 4:15-16).

If, when Paul addressed himself as a father to his disciples, he was doing something forbidden by Jesus, then wouldn't Paul be tempting us to sin?

These aren't odd or isolated references. St. John along with Paul seemed to encourage a filial devotion from his spiritual offspring. At least nine times in his first letter John fondly called his disciples "children" or "little children." Paul called the Galatians "my children" (Gal 4:19) and Timothy "my true child in the faith" (1 Tm 1:2). He pleaded on behalf of Onesimus, "my child, whom I have begotten" (Phlm 10).

How can this be, given Jesus' apparent prohibition? It's not difficult to fathom. The teacher who speaks the living and enduring word of God to us is like a spiritual father playing an essential role in our rebirth in Christ. Discipleship is inseparable from responsible parenthood. A spiritual parent, like a physical parent, is accountable to God for the care and nurture of his children.

That accountability to God was just what the scribes, Pharisees, and rabbis neglected in the exercise of their office. They corrupted the language of spiritual parenthood by insisting on honorific titles as elitist badges that gained them access to privilege, financial advantage, and many perks of lordship over others. When we see similar abuse, we should not adopt or honor such titles.

But if the use of such titles is not always inappropriate, then why does Jesus use such absolute language? Hebrew scholars remind us that the Jews employed the linguistic convention of using absolute contrasts to make comparative points. It's a form of hyperbole.

Jesus, for instance, said if we don't hate our mother and father, we aren't worthy of being his disciple (see Mt 10:37; Lk 14:26; see also Mal 1:2-3). Yet we're also commanded to honor our mother and father (see Ex 20:12; Dt 5:16; Mt 15:4; 19:19; Eph 6:2). How do we reconcile the two apparently contradictory commands?

When our allegiances are challenged and our choices narrowed between obeying God or man, then there is no middle ground. To reinforce the unparalleled priority of God over all creatures, Jesus employed the language of absolute contrast: Love one, hate the other.

The Levites, for example, were commended for executing anyone who worshiped the golden calf, whether the evildoers were Levites, fathers, brothers, or children (see Dt 33:9-11; Ex 32:27-29). Kinship ties were not to prevent the community from stoning family members who enticed others to commit idolatry (see Dt 13:6-10) or a child who struck his parents (see Ex 21:15), cursed them (see Ex 21:17; Lv 20:9), or was incorrigible (see Dt 21:18-21). Faithfulness to God takes precedence over the claims and language of kinship, biological as well as spiritual.

St. John also employed absolute contrast to stress a comparative point: "I write this to you about those who would deceive you; but the anointing which you received from him abides in you, and *you have no need that any one should teach you*, as his anointing teaches you about everything, and is true, and is no lie" (1 Jn 2:26-27, emphasis added).

On the face of it, has anybody written anything more absurd? Here is a teacher warning us against listening to any teacher. Is John mad? Why waste time writing? If his letter were to be taken literally, his readers would disregard his letter!

In context, John is warning against prideful teachers who want to create dependence upon themselves. He paternally reminds the disciples, his "little children" (1 Jn 2:1, 12, 14, 18, 28; 3:7, 18; 4:4; 5:21), that they have an internal witness that is more trustworthy than these false teachers. Obviously, he isn't forbidding all teachers, for that would be tantamount to denying the teaching in his letter.

Jesus' warnings in Matthew 23 about calling men teachers, fathers, masters, leaders, and so on are in a similar vein. They do not utterly prohibit the language of spiritual parentage, but the debasing of such language. Better not to use it at all than to mock God by corrupting it. Jesus uses extreme language to combat extreme abuse.

Aren't annulments just Catholic divorces?

An annulment is just the opposite of a divorce. Divorce tries to break apart what God has joined together; an annulment simply recognizes that God never joined the couple together in the first place.

For many the idea that what one imagined as a real marriage, sometimes enduring for decades, was in fact lacking in key elements is shocking. After all, we think, who knows better than the couple at the altar whether or not they are married? But just as the sick man who is his own doctor has a fool as his physician, so too the husband or wife who thinks he or she defines the conditions of a valid marriage. We are often not the best judges of our own condition.

Marriage is God's idea. It isn't our invention or possession. He, not Romeo and Juliet, Antony and Cleopatra, Oscar Wilde and Lord Alfred Douglas, established the conditions by which we enter into that holy estate which is the sacrament of matrimony.

Given that Christ bestowed the powers of binding and loosing on the Church rather than Caesar (that is, the civil authorities), it's the Church that defines Christian marriage. But here is a little understood fact: the priest doesn't perform the sacrament of marriage. He only "witnesses" the marriage. The husband and wife actually administer the sacrament to one another.

When the Church issues a declaration of nullity, it is saying that it withdraws its witness because it now sees that the conditions necessary for a valid marriage were absent. The couple went through the motions, but there was no marriage. God requires certain commitments from a couple in order to establish their marriage.

When Adam rejoiced over God's gift of Eve by uttering the first love poem, the Scripture followed by saying, "Therefore a man leaves his father and his mother and cleaves to his wife, and they become one flesh" (Gn 2:24; see also 2:23; 1:28). This aphorism gives us some rough guidelines for what constitutes a valid marriage.

Consent. Mature dedication to establish a new family unit.

Permanence. Commitment to a lifelong covenantal union with one's spouse.

Fidelity. Consummation of the union through sexual intercourse with the expectation of children.

In short, the conditions for validity are "leaving," "cleaving," and "becoming one flesh."

Sometimes these conditions or their corollaries are absent in a marriage. We can find this situation at times in Scripture when God set aside invalid marriages (see Gn 21:14; Dt 7:3; Ezr 9,10; Mal 2:10-16). An annulment is simply the recognition by the Church that what appeared to be a valid marriage was actually not. It says nothing about who is the better Christian or whether or not the couple experienced authentic love or who is to blame for the tragic outcome of the relationship. All an annulment determines is that at the time of the wedding one or both parties lacked the ability to give proper consent or, in some way, violated the Church's requirement for marriage. A divorce dissolves a marriage; an annulment says there was no marriage.

What are the grounds for an annulment? Seeking an annulment is a juridical procedure; that is, it partakes of the language of law, not love. Consequently, the vocabulary surrounding annulments sounds terribly contractual rather than covenantal, prosecutorial rather than pastoral. But here goes. Roughly, there are three evidences that any marriage was invalid or "null," hence the terms "annulment" or "declaration of nullity."

- The husband or wife lacked the basic capacity for marriage.
- The husband or wife failed to give sufficient consent to marriage as the Church understands and proclaims it.
- The husband or wife failed to manifest this consent in a proper way, that is, in the proper canonical form.

These "three C's" are to be kept in mind: capacity, consent, canonical form.

Many conditions might—I stress *might*—involve one or more of those big three:

- the attempted marriage of a baptized Catholic to an unbaptized person;
- insufficient age;
- blood relationships closer than second cousin;
- force or grave fear (so-called "shotgun weddings");
- marriage to a stepchild or adopted child;
- inability to exercise adequate discretion;

- unwillingness to bear children;
- murder of a previous spouse in order to get free to remarry;
- a previously existing valid marriage;
- failure to intend lifelong permanence;
- a history of infidelity, mental illness, alcoholism, drug use, duplicity, or deception;
- concealment of some important fact such as impotence or sterility (see Canons 1083-1094, 1103, 1101, 1098).

These are conditions to be considered at the time of original consent to the marital vows. If these conditions develop later, they have no necessary bearing on the capacity to exercise proper consent at the time of the wedding.

A person begins the annulment process by talking with the local priest. He will help in the preparation of the paperwork, the witnesses, and the rigorous self-examination that goes into seeking an annulment. An application is then sent to the diocesan marriage tribunal. The tribunal is competent in canon law and Church teaching and will examine the application.

Someone is appointed as a "Defender of the Bond"—that is, he argues for the validity of the union. The "Promoter of Justice" may intervene in the case if he thinks that the public good is at risk. While civil lawyers are not permitted to participate, someone trained in canon law may present the case.

Costs vary but run between $200 and $1,000, depending on where a person lives. Some dioceses charge a bit more; some charge nothing at all. Those applying for annulment should expect a decision within a year after they complete their self-examination and fill out the application and the witnesses respond.

A civil divorce is usually necessary before filing for an annulment, but not absolutely. The tribunal judges need to verify that reconciliation is impossible, and a civil divorce is normally regarded as important evidence.

People often ask whether an annulment means that the children of such a union are "bastards"? Absolutely not! Since a civil, rather than a Christian, marriage presumably existed, the children are not considered "illegitimate." Even in canon law children born or conceived in a "putative," that is, alleged or assumed, marriage are considered children of a marital union even if in the future it is discovered that the marriage was, strictly speaking, invalid (Canon 1137, 1139, 1061).

Why are annulments easier to get than they used to be? Modern American culture knows more about human psychology and less about what God requires for marriage. The Church is more sensitive to the effects of alcohol, drugs, physical and sexual abuse, and other factors in handicapping a person's ability to truly consent or understand the covenantal significance of Christian marriage.

While people often complain that annulments are more common than they used to be, they also complain that our culture doesn't treasure marriage as highly as it once did. The second leads to the first. In a culture that doesn't stress marriage as an institution of lifelong permanence between a man and a woman, requiring strict fidelity and ordered to the procreation and education of children, we would expect more invalid marriages, since people don't quite know what they are getting into when they pop the question. When they say "I do," they don't necessarily intend the same thing earlier generations intended.

While annulments are deeply misunderstood by the secular media, and Catholics don't help a lot by all our legalistic language, those who have gone through the process testify to its healing power. I have yet to meet a person who, having entered the annulment process, doesn't come away saying how grace freed and equipped them for a future filled with greater self-knowledge, relational sensitivity, spiritual fervor, and a reconciled heart. How powerful a realization that "what therefore God has joined together, let no man put asunder" (Mt 19:6). Likewise, "what God has *not* joined together, let no man coerce as one."

What are holy days of obligation?

Just as ancient Israel had feast days celebrating key events in its history, so too Christ's Church sets aside certain days to commemorate important mysteries revealed by the good news of Jesus Christ.

Sunday, the day of Christ's resurrection, is the foremost and universal "Holy Day of Obligation" on which Christians are to gather together for worship and cease the labors by which they earn their livings. Each Sunday is a little Easter. Grace, sabbath rest, and devotion should mark these days. Catholics "are bound to participate in Mass ... [and] abstain from those labors and business concerns which impede the worship to be rendered to God, the joy which is proper to the Lord's Day, or the proper relaxation of mind and body."[30]

Christmas (December 25) commemorates the Eternal Word's taking on human flesh in the person of Jesus, born of a woman.

The solemnity of Mary, Mother of God, (January 1) acknowledges that Jesus was a real Son of a real mother.

Epiphany (January 6) celebrates the manifestation of Christ to the world in the coming of the magi to worship him.

Ascension (Thursday of the sixth week of Easter) commemorates the final event of Christ's earthly ministry, his rising to heaven to be seated at the right hand of the Father.

Corpus Christi (Thursday after Trinity Sunday) acknowledges the ongoing presence of Christ in the sacrament of the Eucharist.

The feast of St. Joseph (March 19) recognizes the husband of Mary, stepfather of Jesus, as patron saint of the universal Church. He stood watch over the body of Christ as he grew up in Nazareth. He stands watch over the growing body of Christ today.

The feast of Sts. Peter and Paul (June 29) celebrates the two foremost preachers of Christ in the apostolic era.

Assumption (August 15) recognizes that the body Jesus raised from the dead was derived from Mary's bodily substance. In assuming her to heaven at the moment of her passing from this world, he demonstrated the overflowing generosity of his own bodily resurrection.

All Saints (November 1) keeps alive our strong family ties with those members of Christ's body who have passed on but remain in living communion with us.

Immaculate Conception (December 8) celebrates God's victory over the power of sin as he prepared Mary from her conception to be a fit dwelling place for the glory of his Son.

Each bishop's conference can abolish observance of certain holy days or transfer them to a Sunday. The United States bishops, for example, decided not to make the feasts of St. Joseph and Sts. Peter and Paul days of obligation and transferred the solemnities of the Epiphany and Corpus Christi to the nearest Sunday.

What is holy water, and why do Catholics use it?

Holy water is one of many *sacramentals*. Sacramentals are aids to devotion. Sometimes they are objects, such as holy water, scapulars, statues, medals, or rosaries. Sometimes they are actions, such as blessings, exorcisms, or the sign of the cross.

While sacraments objectively confer grace, the value of a sacramental depends on the disposition and openness of the believer to receive grace from God. The number of sacramentals varies, and they can be established or abolished by the pastoral judgment of the Church. The sacraments, on the other hand, were instituted by Christ and cannot be added to or taken from.

Now let's dive into holy water in particular. Water has always played an important symbolic role in biblical faith. Ancient Israel used to purify people and places by sprinkling them with water shaken from a dipped branch of hyssop (see Lv 14:49-52; Nm 19:18; Ps 51:7). Israelite priests ritually washed their hands before and after offering sacrifice. The temple in Jerusalem had fonts for worshippers to cleanse themselves.

The early Christians washed their hands before praying; today, Catholic priests wash their hands at the beginning of the Liturgy of the Eucharist. In the sacrament of baptism, a sacramental (holy water) becomes the material substance used by God to effect the remission of sins.

Plain water becomes holy water through the blessing of a priest. For instance, water is blessed at the Easter Vigil for the baptism of infants and catechumens (those being received into the Church) that night. This "Easter water" remains throughout the Easter season and is used in the Rite of Blessing and sprinkling with holy water at Sunday Mass or for baptism celebrated during this season.

This holy water used to be retained for the entire liturgical year until the next Easter season. For hygienic, as well as theological, reasons we now use fresh water for baptisms outside of the Easter season.

After being blessed, the holy water is placed in a receptacle somewhere accessible to worshippers. Some people hang holy water fonts in their home near the front door. But most of us are familiar with the small holy water fonts that hang on the wall near the entrance of most Catholic churches.

Some churches now have large baptismal fonts that sit in the vestibule. Incoming worshippers can dip their fingers into the font and then make the sign of the cross as a preparation to enter the sacred mysteries. With this sacramental we're reminded of our baptism and union with Christ in his death and resurrection, and we pray to be cleansed and forgiven of any venial sins that have stained us on our journey through the world.

VI. Spirituality and Morality

What is a novena?

Catholic practices are frequently given institutional expression through reflection and action on the smallest details of Scripture. Such is the case with the *novena* (from the Latin word *novem,* "nine"), a nine-day period of prayerful preparation. This prayer tradition finds its template in the nine days of prayerful, expectant waiting of the Blessed Virgin Mary and the apostles between Christ's ascension and the Day of Pentecost.

Novenas can run for nine consecutive days, for nine specific weekdays (such as nine Mondays), or for a particular day in each of nine months (such as nine first Fridays of the month). During a novena, the person praying engages in focused, intensive prayer, usually in accord with a particular form of devotion to the Sacred Heart of Jesus, the Perpetual Help of Mary, or some particular saint whose life embodies a desired quality. For instance, a husband who is trying to remain faithful to his marital vows might pray for strength in a novena dedicated to St. Joseph, the husband of Mary.

Novenas can be private or public. Public novenas normally have specified prayers so that the people can "with one accord devote themselves to prayer" (Acts 1:14; see also 2:1).

Why did the Church send people to hell for not eating fish on Fridays?

At times, certain preachers may have tried to scare the hell out of some folks hoping to scare them out of hell, but the Catholic Church has no authority to send people to hell or even to name people in hell, and it never has. Jesus did invest the leaders of his Church, however, with his authority to "bind and loose" (Mt 16:19; 18:18).

As explained earlier, this was a familiar formula in the first century. The rabbis had the power of making *halakah,* or rules of conduct, for the faith community. These rules included the setting aside of days for fasting and repentance.

Because Friday is the day Christ died for the sin of the world, it carries a special sacred significance for Catholics. To set this day apart, the Church has taught that we are to perform works of penance. Just as it was common in the Old Testament for the leaders of the community to declare national days of fasting in order to demonstrate repentance from their sins, so too is this practice appropriate for the leaders of Christ's New Covenant community.[1]

Canon Law declares:

All Christ's faithful are obliged by divine law, each in his or her own way, to do penance. However, so that all may be joined together in a certain common practice of penance, days of penance are prescribed. On these days the faithful are in a special manner to devote themselves to prayer, to engage in works of piety and charity, and to deny themselves, by fulfilling their obligations more faithfully and especially by observing the fast and abstinence.... Abstinence from meat, or from some other food as determined by the Episcopal Conference, is to be observed on all Fridays, unless a solemnity should fall on a Friday. Abstinence and fasting are to be observed on Ash Wednesday and Good Friday.[2]

Prior to February 17, 1966, generations of Catholics understood the Friday abstinence to mean abstaining from meat, just as Daniel the prophet had done as he mourned over the sins of Israel (see Dn 10:1-3). But Pope Paul VI modified the discipline in his apostolic constitution

Poenitemini. He was concerned that the discipline was degenerating into a formalistic legalism.

For many Catholics, the attitude had become, "TGIF! No meat? No problem—because there are plenty of other ways to party down!" Such an attitude ignores the spirit of the discipline.

The basic purpose of the Friday abstinence is to establish a regular rhythmic and corporate self-denial in which Catholics support and reinforce one another in a vital spiritual discipline. When I was growing up, it wasn't uncommon to find restaurants who made sure their menus included special fish dishes on Friday. Churches often had fish fries. Even today some restaurant chains offer seafood buffets on Friday as a way of appealing to Catholics.

But as Paul VI reminded us, it's not first of all about avoiding filet mignon, but about "prayer-fasting-charity." He urged Catholics to show solidarity with "their brothers who suffer in poverty and hunger, beyond all boundaries of nation and continent."

After *Poenitemini,* each bishops' conference could decide exactly what the culturally appropriate penitential practices should be. For example, in 1984 the French bishops reinstated the Friday abstinence from meat, but also included tobacco and alcohol (over the objections of French winemakers, I'm sure). In America, other forms of penance can be substituted for abstinence from meat.

To consciously and maliciously refuse to participate in this communal discipline is a serious matter. It weakens the witness of the Church to Christ's atoning work on Good Friday and ignores an invitation to the grace offered by Christ. So it's sad that many American Catholics have lost the sense of community that once bound us together in this discipline.

What are relics?

Kevin Orlin Johnson tells the story of a university chaplain who got an excited call in the middle of the night. "Father!" cried an elderly lady of his acquaintance, "is it true that anything handled by a saint is a relic?"

"Why, yes," the priest replied. "Anything we know to have been touched to a saint's body is what you call a third-class relic. Why?"

"Well!" she said proudly, "I was once spanked by Mother Cabrini!"[3]

Biblical people have always revered items associated with holy persons and events. Relics of ancient Israel's past—the manna from the wilderness, Aaron's rod that budded, and the tablets of the law—were all set aside, deposited, and reverenced in the ark of the covenant (see Heb 9:3-4). Scripture favorably describes and nowhere forbids the venerating of relics.

The Bible also shows us that relics can be invested with God's power. Think of the healing hem of Christ's garment touched by a hemorrhaging woman (see Mt 9:19-22). Miracles were worked through the mantle of Elijah and the bones of Elisha (see 2 Kgs 2:13-14; 13:20-21). And "God did extraordinary miracles by the hands of Paul, so that handkerchiefs or aprons were carried away from his body to the sick, and diseases left them and the evil spirits came out of them" (Acts 19:11-12).

Since the early days of the Church the remains of martyrs and holy persons have been called relics, from the Latin *reliquiae,* meaning "remains." A reliquary is a vessel that contains and displays these remains.

The martyr (Greek *martus,* "witness") was celebrated as the disciple who most faithfully imitated Christ in his death. He witnessed by the shedding of his blood at the hands of the enemies of God. His willingness to die for the name of Jesus bore witness, par excellence, to the life of the age to come, a life superior to this world that was passing away. Early Christian worship developed over the gravesites of those who had been martyred, since the martyrs were those who were thought to have been special vehicles of the Holy Spirit.

This association between the martyrs and the altar was already clear by the time the biblical book of Revelation was written: "I saw under the altar the souls of those who had been slain for the word of God and for the witness they had borne; they cried out with a loud voice, 'O Sovereign Lord, holy and true, how long before thou wilt judge and avenge our blood on those who dwell upon the earth?'" (Rv 6:9-10).

Each celebration of the Lord's Supper was a joining in the deaths of Jesus and of those who had literally died with him in martyrdom. St. Ambrose wrote: "They who have been redeemed by his sufferings are beneath the altar," even as Christ's sacrifice was represented on the altar.

As Peter Brown, the preeminent historian of late antiquity, puts it: "At their graves, the eternity of paradise and the first touch of the resurrection come into the present. In the words of St. Victricious of Rouen: here are bodies, where every fragment is 'linked by a bond to the whole stretch of eternity.'"

This was no mere idealizing of the dead. The martyr was an intimate of God who was still a living member of the Church. When his tomb and the Church's altar were joined, the Roman world was jolted.

Graves were now "non-graves," private places were now public, township sites once reserved for the dead were now being inhabited by the living. Cities were growing up on cemeteries. Life was replacing death. A distinctive sign of a growing Christian community in late antiquity was the presence of shrines and relics.

Eventually, when churches were built in territories that had no martyrs, a fragment of a martyr's remains would be embedded in or around the altar. By the Second Council of Nicea in 787, each church building had to contain a relic before it could be consecrated. Today, each Catholic Church contains a relic. According to canon law, "The ancient tradition of keeping the relics of martyrs and other saints under a fixed altar is to be preserved according to the norms given in the liturgical books."[4]

No, Christians weren't worshipping the martyrs. As St. Augustine said: "It is not to any of the martyrs, but to the God of the martyrs, although in memory of the martyrs, that we raise our altars." St. Jerome was equally clear: "We do not worship, we do not adore, for fear that we should bow down to the creature rather than to the Creator, but we venerate the relics of the martyrs in order the better to adore him whose martyrs they are."

Relics are simply mementos, not idols. A brick from the Berlin Wall, a scrap of a Tchaikovsky score, a shard of a clay chalice from ancient Egypt, all receive places of honor in a person's home or library. We are grateful to let such contemporary "relics" stimulate our memories and affections, but we don't worship our mother's grave even though we keep the site manicured. We don't offer sacrifice to our deceased grandfather's violin even though we hang it prominently in our foyer.

And what about that strand of hair from the voluptuous Deborah M. that a fourteen-year-old Al Kresta used to keep in a shoebox along with his baseball cards, old guitar strings, and torn movie tickets? Well, that was veneration of a high degree, but it wasn't worship.

The Church is very cautious in investigating and approving relics. Anyone who makes or knowingly sells, distributes, or displays false relics for veneration incurs *ipso facto* excommunication reserved to the bishops. All relics must be authenticated and can only be publicly displayed if they have supporting documentation.

A first-class relic is the corpse of a saint or any part of it, such as the bones of Elisha. Second-class relics include any object sanctified by close contact with a saint or Our Lord, such as the handkerchief of St. Paul. Third-class relics are objects or cloths touched to either first- or second-class relics.

Some of the most famous relics include the incorruptible body of St. Bernadette Soubirous; the Shroud of Turin; the gray habit worn by St. Francis of Assisi; the bones of St. Peter; a cascade of hair shorn from St. Thérèse of Lisieux when she entered the convent; a Eucharistic host in Lanciano, Italy, that has turned into flesh and five pellets of blood; and the cloak upon which is imprinted the image of Our Lady of Guadalupe.

Sometimes critics claim that if we tallied up all the claimed relics of the true cross, we'd be able to rebuild the ark of Noah. That's not true. All the certifiable relics of the cross recognized by the Church would add up to only a cube of six inches per side.

Such criticism flows from the sometimes silly superstitions that have grown up around relics. It's not too hard to imagine someone saying, "If the prayers of a righteous man have great power, how much more his bones!" (see Jas 5:16).

Abuse of a legitimate practice, however, is no reason to abolish its proper practice. Otherwise, we would abandon prayer, since it leads some people into magical thinking. Along the same lines, all theological discussion would have to end, because it gives people of a certain temper a form of rabid quarrelsomeness.

Relics are one more way that God demonstrates the fitness of the physical world to be a carrier of his grace and mercy.

What does the Church teach about current apparitions of Jesus, Mary, and the saints?

Throughout history, God has granted individuals revelation through dreams, visions, and apparitions ("apparition" is just the noun form of the verb "to appear"). On the Mount of Transfiguration, Moses and Elijah appeared with Jesus in the sight of Sts. Peter, James, and John (see Mt 17:1-8; Mk 9:2-8; Lk 9:28-36). When St. Paul was caught up to the third heaven, otherwise invisible supernatural realities appeared to him (see 2 Cor 12:1-10). Gabriel appeared to Mary to announce the conception of Jesus (see Lk 1:26-38; for examples of other apparitions, see Gn 26:24; Tb 3:16-17; Lk 1:11-20; Acts 9:3-9).

"In many and various ways God spoke of old to our fathers by the prophets; but in these last days he has spoken to us by a Son" (Heb 1:1-2). While God still speaks today, the coming of Jesus was the climax of divine revelation. Consequently, public revelation ceased with the death of the last apostle.

The *Catechism* teaches: "Christian faith cannot accept 'revelations' that claim to surpass or correct the Revelation of which Christ is the fulfillment, as is the case in certain non-Christian religions and also in certain recent sects which base themselves on such 'revelations.'"[5] So the Church rejects the *Quran*, the *Book of Mormon*, the *Course in Miracles*, the *Urantia* book, the *Ascended Master Discourses*, or any of thousands of purported revelations over the last nineteen hundred years.

Nevertheless, God still sheds light on the revelation given in Christ and through the apostles. The Church investigates claims to supernatural private revelation, and the great minds and hearts of saints such as Augustine, Thomas Aquinas, Teresa of Avila, and John of the Cross have spilled much ink refining the Church's thinking on these matters.

But even when private revelations are recognized by the authority of the Church, "they do not belong ... to the deposit of faith. It is not their role to improve or complete Christ's definitive Revelation, but to help live more fully by it in a certain period of history."[6]

Consequently, only those who are personally convinced that these private revelations are of supernatural origin are obliged to believe in them. Otherwise, Catholics are free to accept or reject them based on prudence.

Apparitions can be diabolical or fraudulent.[7] Discernment is necessary. Christians are also forbidden from seeking out mediums or trying to manipulate supernatural powers to divine the future. The *Catechism* declares:

> All forms of *divination* are to be rejected: recourse to Satan or demons, conjuring up the dead or other practices falsely supposed to "unveil" the future.[8] Consulting horoscopes, astrology, palm reading, interpretation of omens and lots, the phenomena of clairvoyance, and recourse to mediums all conceal a desire for power over time, history, and, in the last analysis, other human beings, as well as a wish to conciliate hidden powers. They contradict the honor, respect and loving fear that we owe to God alone.[9]

This is why the sound judgment of the Church is necessary to discern whether or not a claimed supernatural phenomenon is of God, nature, man, or the devil.

How does the Church approve an apparition?

It engages in empirical, rational, moral, and theological investigation. From the beginning the apostolic Church assumed responsibility for investigating new manifestations of the Spirit and the formation of communities that grew up in response to unusual supernatural phenomena (see Acts 8:14-17; 10:19-11:18; 15:1-35; Gal 2:1-10). The local bishop usually has the task of investigating allegedly supernatural claims, and his is normally the last word as far as the Church is concerned. While the pope can overturn the judgment, he is unlikely to do so unless there are some extenuating circumstances.

The bishop looks at three basic areas: the content of the message (1 Thes 5:19-21); the means by which the message was transmitted, such as trances, ecstasies, voices, visions, and so on; and the character of the spiritual fruit displayed in the life of those influenced by the message (see Mt 7:15-20; 12:22-37).

He might assemble a commission to investigate. He may close the apparition site for a while and call in diverse experts in moral and dogmatic theology, forensic pathology, optics, photography, medicine, abnormal psychology, chemistry, physics—even meteorology, if weather conditions significantly played into the claims. Can this phenomenon be explained away as natural or perhaps even diabolical?

The investigators interview the seers. Is there evidence of hallucinations, grandiosity, schizophrenia, or self-delusion? Inquiries regarding the character of the visionaries are made among their friends, families, acquaintances, spiritual directors, and pastors, as well as those who have attended any public sessions where supernatural manifestations allegedly occurred. Devotion, however, is no guarantee that a revelation isn't false.

The investigators handle and evaluate the artifacts associated with the phenomenon. They gauge the moral and spiritual impact on the seers and the proponents of the apparition. They pore over any alleged messages from Christ, Mary, or the saints to see whether these messages contradict Sacred Tradition, including Scripture, or are internally incoherent and illogical. They scrutinize any claims of healing.

It's important to keep apparitions and other special supernatural manifestations in perspective. St. John of the Cross wryly observed, "One act done in charity is more precious in God's sight than all the visions and communications possible—since they imply neither merit nor demerit—and many who have not received these experiences are incomparably more advanced than others who have had many."

Normally, the local bishop's disapproval buries the claim. In the case of St. Joan of Arc, however, the bishop's decision was reversed. The current apparitions at Medjugorje (1981 and continuing) have faced strong and repeated rejection by the local bishop. Other prominent theologians and churchmen, however, have disputed the bishop's judgment. A definitive decision in this case is probably far off.

After looking at all the facts, the bishop's commission may conclude that these particular private revelations are "probable." Usually that's about as much "approval" as they will give. Nobody is required to believe these apparitions as a matter of divine revelation. At best they are just "probable."

As Pope Benedict XIV said: "Even though many of these revelations have been approved, we cannot and ought not give them the assent of divine faith, but only that of human faith, according to the dictates of prudence whenever these dictates enable us to decide that they are probable and worthy of pious credence."

The approval of a private revelation may be simply "negative"— that is, there is nothing against faith and morals in the revelation or the phenomena emanating from it. People are free to believe it; it is "worthy of belief."

Some of the best known approved apparitions include these:
- the pregnant Virgin of Guadalupe (1531)
- the Miraculous Medal (1830)
- Our Lady of La Salette (1846)
- the Immaculate Conception (Lourdes, 1858)
- Our Lady of Knock (1879)
- Our Lady of Fatima (1917)

Claims of apparitions usually spawn more claims. Soon after the manifestations in Lourdes, for instance, over two hundred apparitions were reported. None were ever taken seriously.

Why don't Catholics use artificial contraception?

Until the Anglican Lambeth Conference of 1930, all Christian traditions shared the Catholic conviction that contracepted intercourse was "immoral." Today, contraception is usually welcomed by most non-Catholics (as well as many Catholics unmindful of the Church's teaching) as a right of Christian liberty or a matter of personal conscience.

Sex is not a peripheral issue. Christ teaches through his Church that all acts of marital intercourse should be open to the transmission of new life—that is, the couple should never take any positive action to disconnect their covenantal love from its life-giving potential. Couples need not have as many children as possible and are expected to weigh their ability to nurture and educate their children. Abstinence during fertile periods is morally permissible.

Further, sexual intercourse in marriage is not just about making babies. Marital intercourse is laden with two meanings, inextricably woven together: life and love, babies and bonding, procreation and interpersonal intimacy. Any attempt to rip apart these meanings is to do violence to what God has joined together in the act of sexual inter-course. We believe in neither loveless life or lifeless love.[10]

To figure out what a book is about, sometimes it helps to look at the first chapter and the last. Scripture begins with the "wedding" of Adam and Eve and the command to be fruitful, multiply, and fill the earth (see Gn 2:18-25). It ends with the "wedding supper of the Lamb," that is, the marriage of Christ and his Church (see Rv 19:9). Salvation history can thus be understood as God wooing a beloved in order to "marry" us so that we might share his most intimate and abundant life for all eternity.

Marriage and sexual intercourse are supposed to make this mystery visible and concrete for us. Scripture paints marriage as a sacramental sign of Christ's love for his Church. We are called to reveal the rela-tionship Christ has with His Church. So in the covenant of marriage the parties share not merely their goods but their very selves. We don't reserve any part of ourselves from the other.

Contraception, however, contradicts this total self-giving. It says: "I give you all of myself except my fertility." As philosopher and moral theologian Janet Smith has put it, it's like saying: "You know I want to make love to you but you are having a bad hair day and I'm having difficulty looking at you. Would you mind putting this bag over your head? I love you, but I don't want to deal with a very important part of you today."

The difference between "I want to have sex with you" and "I want to have a baby with you" is profound. "I want to have sex with you" is on a par with "I want to have dinner with you" or "I want to play ten-nis with you." No big deal.

"I want to have a baby with you" means "I want to be with you from now till forever. I want to bring another one of you into the world, an immortal soul that resembles you. I want all of you, and I want to give you all of me."

In 1968, Pope Paul VI reaffirmed the Church's teaching on marital intercourse in his encyclical *Humanae Vitae.* What we now call the sexual revolution had just begun. The pill was widely available. Pop music and films were beginning to push the limits of decency. The Pope warned that the widespread use of contraceptives would "lead to conjugal infidelity and the general lowering of morality."

I remember 1968. Four years before, the Beatles had innocently sung "I Want to Hold Your Hand." A year before, the Rolling Stones had sung, "Let's spend the night together." But Ed Sullivan and mainstream morality still had enough leverage to force them to sing, "Let's spend some time together."

By 1981, mainstream culture had become so desensitized to casual sex that a wholesome Olivia Newton John could sing "Let's Get Physical." By 1987 all restraints were off, and George Michael sang "I Want Your Sex." By 1994, Nine Inch Nails' refrains described the marital act in the worst of four-letter obscenities and with reference to animals.

Paul VI also warned that widespread acceptance of contraception would place "a dangerous weapon in the hands of those public authorities." Today some Third World countries perform involuntary sterilizations. China has forced abortion for those who exceed their one-child limit, while France and Germany have established incentives for people to have more children because these countries are dangerously underpopulated.

You need not be a Catholic to look upon the enormous rise in divorce, abortion, out-of-wedlock pregnancy, and sexually transmitted disease and recognize that Pope Paul VI foresaw our future more than thirty years ago. What did he know that others didn't?

He knew enough to ask: "What is the purpose of sexual expression?" On the basis of Scripture and Sacred Tradition we know that procreation and intimacy between husband and wife are the inextricable ends of the marital act.

Sometimes people say, "Come on, isn't sex really for pleasure?" Sex is certainly pleasurable, but pleasure isn't the purpose of sex any more than pleasure is the purpose of eating or sleeping.

God often attaches pleasure to activities he knows are vital for our flourishing, such as eating, sleeping, and exercising. But while pleasure accompanies these activities, they are not the *purpose* of these activities—that is, their natural end. For instance, if a person eats merely for pleasure, he is ignoring the purpose of eating, which is nutrition. He may become obese or anorexic or bulimic. We call these illnesses eating "disorders" because they frustrate eating from achieving its natural end.

Paul VI knew that modern culture was ignoring the purpose, the natural end, of sex and that this would lead to chaos and disorder. The recent rise in sexual addiction and deviancy demonstrates what happens when sex is disconnected from its fundamental meaning. As Freud said: "It is a characteristic common to all the perversions that in them reproduction as an aim is put aside."

A world that prates on endlessly about sex, even as it seeks more intense orgasms and more frequent sexual encounters, needs to invite God into the bedroom if it wants to find satisfying, maximum, or even apocalyptic sex. The ancient rabbis used to say that acts of conception should involve three participants: husband, wife, and Holy Spirit. No *ménage à trois* is as intense as that in which the Holy Spirit is invited as the third Party to animate our lovemaking. Sex is not merely good; it's sacred, because it's life-giving!

Isn't Scripture silent on artificial contraception?

While Scripture does not explicitly address the issue of artificial contraception, it forcefully challenges many of the negative attitudes towards children expressed in influential strains of our popular culture. This "contraceptive mentality" includes a bias against conception; a closed rather than open attitude towards the bearing of children; a subtle resentment of large families as alien, even as a threat, to our culture; and the belief that conception is a purely biological phenomenon. The language of Scripture surrounding conception, pregnancy, and large families differs from contemporary Western attitudes as much as life differs from death.

Film critics tell us that a character's first mention or entrance usually reveals something important. So too in Scripture. At the birth of the first child, Eve tells us where babies come from: "I have gotten a man with the help of the Lord" (Gn 4:1).

When the angel of the Lord counsels Hagar, Abraham's exiled servant-wife, he says on God's behalf, "I will so greatly multiply your descendants that they cannot be numbered for multitude" (Gn 16:10). The promise to Abraham is similar: "I ... will multiply you exceedingly" (Gn 17:2).

While we don't deny secondary causal forces, ultimately it is God who controls conception and birth.[11] Who works through the womb? It's an open-and-shut case: the Lord. "Your wife will be like a fruitful vine within your house; your children will be like olive shoots around your table. Lo, thus shall the man be blessed who fears the Lord.... Lo, sons are a heritage from the Lord, the fruit of the womb a reward. Like arrows in the hand of a warrior are the sons of one's youth. Happy is the man who has his quiver full of them!" (Ps 128:3-4; 127:3-5).

So often people say, "We only want two children," or worse, "We don't intend to have children." But if God offered us the blessing of financial prosperity or good health, would we say, "Great, but don't overdo it"?

Onan was commanded to have sexual intercourse with his dead brother's widow in order to raise up children in his name. Technically, this is called a "levirate marriage," from the Latin *levir*, meaning "brother-in-law." It was a common cultural practice in the ancient Middle East and a legal obligation in ancient Israel because it guaranteed social stability for the widow and insured descendants to perpetuate the family line.

Onan, knowing the offspring would not be his, engaged in sexual intercourse but withdrew at the point of ejaculation and spilled his seed on the ground. What he did was displeasing to the Lord, who then took his life as a punishment for his sin (see Gn 38:8-10).

Throughout the centuries, Catholic, Orthodox, and Protestant teachers commonly used this verse to condemn various forms of contraception and masturbation. Martin Luther, for instance, commented: "We call it unchastity, yes, a Sodomite sin. For Onan ... lies with her and copulates, and when it comes to the point of insemination, spills the semen, lest the woman conceive. Surely at such a time the order of nature established by God in procreation should be followed."

Over the last two generations many scholars have argued that Onan displeased God not because he contracepted but because he disobeyed the law to raise up children in his dead brother's name. Fair enough. This is certainly the fundamental disobedience.

However, the punishment for refusing to raise up a child for one's deceased brother was public humiliation, not death (see Dt 25:5-10). Why then was Onan put to death? Because he not only refused to raise up children in his brother's name, but also deceived the community by engaging in a disordered form of sexual intercourse through practicing *coitus interruptus* and spilling his seed.

Compare the biblical rhetoric on children and fruitful intercourse with that of current Western culture, and gauge how far we have come in discounting God's involvement in conception, discrediting children as an unalloyed blessing from God, and disconnecting sexual intercourse from its natural end of producing children.

Parents of large families are regularly treated to rude remarks such as, "Don't you know when to stop?" Rather than a celebration of large families, there is a suspicion of too many children. Many think of children the way the rabbi in the musical *Fiddler on the Roof* thought of the Russian Czar when he prayed: "God bless and keep the Czar—far away from us!"

Listen carefully to the language: Some say, "I got pregnant by accident." Now you can fall down an elevator shaft, get hit by lightning, or swallow a tooth by accident, but you don't get pregnant by accident! Getting pregnant means something went right with sexual intercourse, not that something went wrong. But for many, getting pregnant means something went wrong. I'm reminded of the Alaskan tour guide who, when the sun finally came out after long days of gray, said, "We have some cloud failure."

Consider the vocabulary describing contraceptives. We have the "barrier" methods, which metaphorically communicate that "I need to put something between you and me before we make love. I want to make sure our love doesn't create life. We need to wall off that possibility."

The language of "barriers," "barricades," and "shields," is about war and self-protection rather than love and self-giving. "Spermicides" may not lead to homicide, but they certainly destroy. Even as clinical a term as "the pill" implies that pregnancy is an illness to be inoculated against.

Further, "the pill" works by destroying female fertility and deceiving a woman's body into thinking it is already pregnant so that she stops ovulating. If that doesn't work, then it stops implantation of the conceived child. In other words, when it fails in its task of deception, it kills the victim. Rather than regarding fertility as God's endowment of our creation as embodied souls, the vocabulary of contraception teaches that fertility is a defect to be eliminated.

While Scripture may not address the issue of contraceptive inter-course directly, its portrayal of children and pregnancy argues weightily against artificial conception control. Besides, this interpretation of the Bible was an unchallenged part of Christian tradition until the twentieth century.

VII. Angels, Mary, and the Other Saints

What does the Catholic Church teach about angels?

Angels are incorporeal beings—that is, they don't have physical bodies. They are invisible. They are spirits.

Angels are visitors from beyond this material universe and are not composed of energy or matter or radiant light or ectoplasm or any material substance. Further, "as purely spiritual creatures angels have intelligence and will: they are personal and immortal creatures, surpassing in perfection all visible creatures, as the splendor of their glory bears witness."[1]

How do we know they exist if they have no bodies? Well, we know many things that are not extended in space: laws of logic, the concept of the good, the idea of a triangle, the notion of "two." Immaterial things aren't unreal; they're just intangible. So we know of angels through divine revelation, the consistent teaching of Christ's Church, as well as the striking stories told by those who claim to have encountered them.

Throughout Sacred Scripture the existence of angels is taken for granted rather than expressly argued (see, for example, Dn 12:1; Tb 5:4-7; Is 6:2; Mt 1:20; Acts 5:19; Heb 2:9). In Greek and Hebrew, *angel* is a rather colorless word and simply means a human or heavenly "messenger," rather than something magnificent such as "winged one" or "flaming breath" or "sparkly companion."

While angels are immaterial and don't reside in this world, they do visit these parts. They are task-oriented creatures. God sends them with a message from beyond this world, and when they deliver their messages they sometimes appear to the addressee in a manner that inspires awe. The invisible world has penetrated the visible, and a crisis occurs.

"Fear not" is often the greeting of an angel. We're not moved to cuddle them like cocker spaniels but to fall back from them in shock. And why not? They are glorious aliens from another order of existence who worship in the presence of God and who cooperate with him in the governing of the cosmos.[2]

At this point, I should try to correct a common misconception perpetuated in movies, pop spirituality, and books on alleged angelic encounters. Angels are not disembodied human souls. Upon death, human beings do not become angels. Human beings are a spirit-body compound. We have a soul, but upon death we await the resurrection of our bodies. Only then is our redemption complete.

On the other hand, angels, as pure spirits, cannot possess a body. To put it simply, human souls are meant for bodies; angels are not. We are different species. In fact, at the end of time, according to St. Paul, we will judge the fallen angels (see 1 Cor 6:3).

Why do Catholics believe in guardian angels?

On October 2 Catholics celebrate the Feast of the Guardian Angels because every individual has a guardian angel, and awareness of our guardian angel can be a comfort and aid in our spiritual growth. The *Catechism* quotes St. Basil when it teaches: "Beside each believer stands an angel as protector and shepherd leading him to life."[3]

This seems a common-sense implication from many passages of Scripture. For instance, "For he will give his angels charge of you to guard you in all your ways. On their hands they will bear you up, lest you dash your foot against a stone. You will tread on the lion and the adder, the young lion and the serpent you will trample under foot" (Ps 91:11-13).

Such angelic personal care shows up time and again. The Hebrew heroine Judith proclaimed, "His angel hath been my keeper both going hence, and abiding there, and returning from thence hither" (Jdt 13:20, Douay).

In the New Testament, the task of angels as "ministering spirits sent forth to serve, for the sake of those who are to obtain salvation" (Heb 1:14) is revealed even more clearly than in the Old Testament (see for example Lk 1-3; Acts 10:3; Rv 7:11ff).

When Jesus urges us to develop the trust and unpretentiousness of little children and then warns those who would despoil the souls of these little ones, he concludes with what may seem to us a curious statement: "See that you do not despise one of these little ones, for I tell you that in heaven their angels always behold the face of my Father who is in heaven" (Mt 18:10). Each of these children has his or her own angel before God in heaven.

Christ's original audience wouldn't have found the reference puzzling. Jesus was drawing on the Hebrew revelation that angels are guardians of nations and individuals, adults as well as children, and they perform various assignments.

God casts each human person in a dramatic story of redemption. The future of the universe hinges on our choices. He has discharged guardian angels to assist us in our roles.

Referring to Christ's words above, St. Jerome commented, "How great the dignity of the soul, since each one has from his birth an angel commissioned to guard it." St. Thomas further taught that our guardian angels could act upon our senses and imagination, though not upon our will. He added that they would also remain with us after our final union with God.

I suspect that many people dismiss guardian angels not because they've examined the data of Scripture or considered how eternity might penetrate time, but because of an adolescent prejudice:

Guardian angels look like "imaginary friends" who are just projections of our own need for consolation in an unsafe world. But the fact that some spiritually stunted people find comfort in the notion is no argument against the actual existence of guardian angels.

It's like saying that because a frightened child finds peace in the notion that the police are watching over him while he sleeps, then police don't exist. Why shouldn't other rational spirits share the same space as we do?

Why do Catholics make so much of Mary?

In one word: Jesus. As the *Catechism* teaches: "What the Catholic faith believes about Mary is based on what it believes about Christ, and what it teaches about Mary illumines in turn its faith in Christ.... Mary's role in the Church is inseparable from her union with Christ and flows directly from it."[4] All the Marian dogmas originate, first of all, as statements illumining the real identity of Christ.[5]

Catholics make so much of Mary because we make so much of the Divine Person she conceived, bore, nurtured, taught, raised, and proclaimed, and for whom she suffered the grief of a mother's loss of a child. Whereas all patriarchs, prophets, kings, apostles, evangelists, martyrs, fathers, doctors, priests, and bishops bore *witness* to the Word, she literally *bore* the Word. Among creatures, she is in a class by herself, and "all generations will call [her] blessed" (Lk 1:48). Or as the medieval Italian poet Dante put it: She is "more humble yet more exalted than any other creature."

Since Jesus honors his mother, so do those who imitate him. Our appreciation of Mary is proportioned to our esteem for Christ. If we worship the Son, we will certainly honor the mother.

Catholics also make so much of Mary because her life is rife with lessons in discipleship. While Jesus is our Master, Mary is his model disciple.

She's an active listener to God's word and keeps it. As Gabriel announces that she will be with child out of wedlock, a potentially capital crime, she doesn't hesitate or dispute. She asks a simple question designed to identify more precisely how she is to carry out the word she has just heard: "How can this be since I have no husband?"

When Mary receives the supernatural promise that her pregnancy will be the work of the Holy Spirit, she relies on that promise: "Let it be to me according to your Word" (see Lk 1:34-45). Her quick assent reveals a character honed by regular obedience in the small details of life.

Mary is a type of the ideal disciple because she receives God's Word and Spirit in such a full way that Christ is literally and concretely formed within her. As the one who is most visibly and tangibly impregnated by the divine Word, she is also the one who most visibly and tangibly acts out our responsibility to transmit the Savior to the world. While the Holy Spirit has poured out God's love into our hearts, the Holy Spirit has poured out God's love into her womb. She is the one whom Jesus commends: "Blessed rather are those who hear the word of God and keep it" (Lk 11:28).

Mary is also a model of prayer, praise, and meditation. After St. Elizabeth confirms the great things God is doing in Mary's life, what Mary sings forth in praise and prayer we call the "Magnificat": "My soul magnifies the Lord, and my spirit rejoices in God, my Savior" (Lk 1:46-47). When the shepherds leave after telling her what the angels had told them about the birth of her child, she "kept all these things, pondering them in her heart" (Lk 2:19). Mary thus not only receives God's word and does it; she reflects on it and prays it.

She is also a heroic model for those who suffer. She is Our Lady of Sorrows, whose feast is commemorated on September 15. Simeon warned that her Son would be "set for the fall and rising of many in Israel, and for a sign that is spoken against (and a sword will pierce through your own soul also), that thoughts out of many hearts may be revealed" (Lk 2:34-35).

Thirty years later, she stood, not swooned, at the foot of the cross, witnessing the death of her Son condemned as a common criminal. Suffering had marked her life: a problem pregnancy, no room at the inn, the flight into Egypt, a "runaway" Son stigmatized by his family as mentally unstable, and the death of this, her only Son. So much original promise, so little to show for it at the moment of crucifixion. When the centurion thrust the sword into Christ's side, a sword pierced her own soul, just as Simeon had predicted.

Mary is an essential part of salvation history: "[W]hen the time had fully come, God sent forth his Son, born of woman, born under the law, to redeem those who were under the law, so that we might receive adoption as sons. And because you are sons, God has sent the Spirit of his Son into our hearts, crying, 'Abba, Father!'" (Gal 4:4-6).

We are adopted into the family of God. We celebrate the love of the Father, the mission of the Son, the gift of the Spirit, the maternal role of the woman from whom the Redeemer was born, and our own divine sonship.

Marian devotion is proportioned to our appreciation of Christ. As Venerable John Henry Newman once said: "I don't suppose we can love our lady too much as long as we love our Lord a great deal more." Or as Blessed John XXIII remarked: "The Madonna is not pleased when she is put above her Son."

Do Catholics worship Mary and the other saints?

No. Only the Trinity is to be "worshipped" as the word is commonly used in English today.

In the old wedding service of the *Anglican Book of Common Prayer,* however, the husband would say to the wife, "With my body I thee worship." Magistrates or other civil authorities were once addressed as "Your worship." That's because in earlier times, "worship" simply meant to declare someone's or something's proper worth.

In those days, then, to address someone as "Your worship" was simply to say "You worthy one." Some of the older Catholic devotional literature referred to the worship of Mary or the saints in this older sense. In Catholic doctrine, however, there is always a bright, shining dividing line between *latria*—that is, the adoration that belongs to the uncreated Trinity alone—and *dulia*—the honor due to the excellence of created persons such as the saints.

Mary receives *hyperdulia,* which means, we might say, just a whole lot more *dulia.* The Second Vatican Council mentions that this veneration of Mary "as it has always existed in the Church, for all its uniqueness, differs essentially from the cult of adoration, which is offered equally to the Incarnate Word and to the Father and the Holy Spirit and it is most favorable to it."[6] God alone is to be worshipped in this latter sense.

We regularly give out Oscars, diplomas, and Olympic medals to honor excellence in film, education, and athletics. Honoring, esteeming, or venerating creatures for their achievements and character in no wise distracts us from giving to God the adoration and worship he deserves. One might even argue that the refusal to honor properly such creaturely excellences leaves a void in modern life that is filled by a cult of celebrity. Rather than honoring the bones of a martyr, we scramble to claim a slip of Princess Diana's hair.

Catholics do not believe that God is parsimonious in sharing his glory. He made us in his image and intended his glory to be reflected through his creatures. A dubious logic argues, "If God alone is all-glorious, then no one else is glorious at all. No exaltation may be admitted for any creature, since this endangers the exclusive prerogative of God. God shares his glory with no one!"

Jesus, however, corrects this misunderstanding as he prays to his Father: "The glory which thou hast given me I have given to them [the disciples] that they may be one even as we are one." God's glory rests on Jesus, and through Jesus on his followers (see Jn 17:1, 22). When this glory in God's people is seen, others are drawn to God, not diverted from God.

The principle is not hard to understand: the glory of a king is revealed in the glory of his court. The greater the king, the greater those who surround him at court. As Thomas Howard has put it:

What king surrounds himself with warped, dwarfish, worthless creatures? The more glorious the king, the more glorious are the titles and honors he bestows. The plumes, cockades, coronets, diadems, mantles, and rosettes that deck his retinue testify to one thing alone: his own majesty and munificence. He is a very great king, to have figures of such immense dignity in his train, or even better, to have raised them to such dignity. These great lords and ladies, mantled and crowned with the highest possible honor and rank, are precisely his vassals. This glittering array is his court! All glory to him and, in him, glory and honor to these others.[7]

I have an artist friend whose wonderful and awe-inspiring exhibitions I have often attended. Is Chuck Gillies upset when I lavish my praise on his works? Of course not! He accepts such praise as a personal honor. In the same way, we honor God when we praise his works.

Does the artist feel threatened or denigrated when we praise him for the works of his hands? Does the king suspect he is being undermined or belittled when we are caught up praising the magnificence of his court? Mary and the other saints are the artistry of God. They are courtiers in the court of the King. They deserve to be honored and venerated. And we come to know God better as we admire his glory shining through the creatures he has made and redeemed.

Why do Catholics call Mary the Mother of God?

A thing can sometimes be too close to be seen. Mary did not originate God as human women gave birth to gods in some pagan religions. But she did "mother" him. As with all Marian questions, we should come back to the most fundamental theological question for Christians: Who is Jesus? Did he have a mother? What should she be called?

Scripture is explicit on this point. When the pregnant Mary goes to visit her kinswoman, Elizabeth greets her by saying, "And why is this granted me, that the mother of my Lord should come to me?" (Lk 1:43).

In her womb, Mary is carrying Elizabeth's Lord, the God of Israel, the great I AM. He is nourished by Mary's blood, food, and oxygen. *In utero* he listens and learns the beating of her heart and the rhythm of her breathing. Soon he will long for her lactating breasts and the sunshine of her smile. He is Son; she is mother.

It's really very simple. Mary is truly Jesus' mother. She had no less a maternal relationship with Jesus than our birth mothers have with us. Out of her own body's substance she donated the genetic material that formed Jesus' body in the womb. She was the sole human donor of his

DNA. Since he did not have a human father, Mary gave him the body that the Father would eventually raise from the dead.

But a mother provides much more than our protoplasm. She also imbues us with personality and forms our first human relationship. From our mothers we learn to walk, repeat the alphabet, use eating utensils, and share our toys. From our mothers we learn the truths of the faith, values, morals, habits, reading, writing, manners, and respect and love for others, including our mother.

We love our mothers, and our mothers love us. Our mothers are woven into our lives not only biologically but psychologically, spiritually, personally, and relationally. So then:

Premise #1. Mary is the real mother of a real Son.

Premise #2. Jesus was truly God.

Conclusion: Mary is truly the mother of God.

Some theologians in the fifth century argued that the Virgin Mary gave birth only to Christ's human nature, not his divine nature. The Church concluded at the Council of Ephesus (431), however, that a mother does not give birth to a nature, she bears a person. The Virgin Mary bore the divine Person, Jesus Christ, not just an abstract set of properties we call a "human nature." She was indeed the *Theotokos,* the God-bearer, which is the favored Eastern Orthodox term for Mary, affirming the fact of her divine maternity.

Sometimes people refer to Mary as a mere vessel. Vessel, yes. "Mere"? No.

The Virgin Mary was not some impersonal bit of necessary obstetrical equipment, a piece of medical apparatus, a vaginal conduit or gynecological pipeline so Jesus could slide down from heaven like a penny dropped down a chute. She was and is a person, a genuine mother, who cooperated with the grace of God in ushering the Savior into the world. She is the only one who can say, "I donated my flesh to God. When God took on human flesh, it was my flesh he took on."

In Hebrews 10:5 we hear Jesus speaking to the Father: "Sacrifices and offering thou hast not desired, but a body hast thou prepared for me." Just what kind of body? What kind of flesh did she donate to Jesus? Was it flesh tainted by original sin?

These questions lead us to consider Mary's Immaculate Conception. What kind of body did God prepare for Jesus?

What is the Immaculate Conception?

The dogma of the Immaculate Conception teaches the truth that "the most Blessed Virgin Mary was, from the first moment of her conception, by a singular grace and privilege of almighty God and by virtue of the merits of Jesus Christ, Savior of the human race, preserved immune from all stain of original sin." By the grace of God, Mary also remained free of even personal sin her whole life.[8]

In that one dense sentence, Pope Pius IX teaches at least three truths about the Immaculate Conception of Mary (not to be confused with the virginal conception of Jesus):

First, Mary did need a savior (see Lk 1:47).

Second, her savior was Jesus Christ through his work on the cross.

Third, Mary was in fact saved from sin, although in a way that's different from the way the rest of us are saved. But her salvation remained a work of God, not a work of Mary.

Some Christians object: "How can you say she needs a savior if she never sinned?" We can be saved "from" as well as saved "out of." She was *preserved* from sin, while we are *delivered* out of it.

Even among our acquaintances we can observe this principle. Some of our fellow Christians have been delivered from sin when they turned away from pornography, alcoholism, embezzlement, or murderous rage. Others, however, never developed a taste for these vices. By the grace of God, they reject such sins habitually because of a virtuous upbringing or a natural self-control. They are saved *from* these things rather than delivered *out* of them.

Two illustrations adapted from medieval theologians make this point. First, a person could be saved from a disease by the healing treatment of a doctor. Yet he could also be saved from the illness by following the doctor's advice before contracting it, thus avoiding the disease entirely. Preventive medicine is to be preferred to curative medicine.

As a second illustration, imagine two travelers strolling down a forest lane. Before them lies a camouflaged pit. The first traveler falls into the pit and is rescued by the local sheriff. The second traveler approaches the pit, and just before she topples in, the sheriff's hand reaches out and pulls her back from the edge. Both travelers needed a savior to save them from the pit.

In Scripture, we see that those whom God selects for a mission of particular importance are sometimes sanctified—that is, set apart—from their mother's womb, as in the case of Jeremiah, John the Baptist, and Paul (see Jer 1:5; Lk 1:15, 41; Gal 1:15). Since Mary was to play an utterly unique role in salvation history, she would require a sanctification proportionate to her calling. Consequently, Mary was "saved" from original sin at the moment of her conception; that's why Gabriel could address her as "full of grace" (Lk 1:28).

But why did Mary have to be free of original sin?

First, God needed to take on a sin-free human nature. He willed that the Second Person of the Trinity would have a human mother and not be formed out of mother earth, as the first Adam had been. What kind of human nature would he receive from this human mother?

Would it be one stained by sin? What would she contribute out of her own life to her son?

Mary donated to Jesus the untainted humanity she had received from God. Jesus derived his unsullied human nature from his mother. The Eternal Son, as Newman put it, "imbibed, he sucked up her blood and her substance into his Divine Person. He became man from her."

When the eternal God took on human flesh, it was Mary's flesh with which he draped himself. It was a body fit for a King.

Fr. Alfred McBride tells the story of a Catholic boy who started telling an older man—a university professor—about Mary's special graces. The professor smiled at the boy's enthusiasm and tried to disarm him by saying, "But there is no difference between her and my mother." The confident boy replied, "You may think so, but let me tell you, there is an enormous difference between the sons."

Mary's sanctification from her mother's womb was a necessary preparation for her maternity of Jesus. The dogma of the Immaculate Conception, like all the Marian dogmas, is first of all about Jesus Christ.[9]

Here's a second reason why the Immaculate Conception was necessary. Before the coming of Christ, God's holy presence traumatized those who were exposed to it. Moses, for example, had to take off his sandals to walk on holy ground. "You cannot see my face, for man shall not see me and live," God told Moses. The people couldn't even touch the foot of Mount Sinai during the giving of the Law without risking death (see Ex 3:5; 19:12-13; 33:20).

As the angelic beings called seraphim covered their faces and sang, "Holy, holy, holy is the Lord of hosts," Isaiah saw the Lord in the temple and was reduced to despair: "Woe is me! For I am lost [I prefer the older English translation here: "undone"]; for I am a man of unclean lips, and I dwell in the midst of a people of unclean lips; for my eyes have seen the King, the Lord of hosts" (Is 6:3, 5).

He was undone—that is, disintegrating—in the presence of the High and Holy One who inhabits eternity and whose Presence was filling the Temple. Isaiah's lips had to be purified by a flaming coal before he could proclaim God's holy word (see verses 6-7). Such close encounters with God led to trauma!

In the days of King David in ancient Israel, during the procession of the ark of the covenant back to Jerusalem, the temple worker Uzzah instinctively reached out to steady this holiest object of Israel when it appeared as though it might tip over. But God struck him dead, because the people were not to "touch the holy things, lest they die" (Nm 4:15; 2 Sm 6:6-7).

Jesus Christ is that Holy One of all eternity. As the angel Gabriel announced to Mary: "The Holy Spirit will come upon you, and the power of the Most High will overshadow you; therefore the child to be born will be called holy, the Son of God" (Lk 1:35).

If Isaiah disintegrated in the presence of the Holy One; if Uzzah was struck dead for touching the holy ark of the covenant; then how long would Mary have lasted if this Holy One of all eternity had taken up residence in a sin-stained womb? She wouldn't merely have expired; she'd have evaporated.

So Mary becomes a hinge figure in the history of holiness. She is the one in whom the holy God of Israel dwelt more intimately than he ever did in any tabernacle, temple or ark. If the Mosaic tabernacle in which God would dwell had to be made perfect, according to the pattern from heaven (see Ex 25:9, 40; 39:32, 42-43), how much more so Mary, the tabernacle of the Incarnate Word?

Because of her Immaculate Conception, she was able to act as a "step-down transformer," so to speak, reducing the trauma of our encounter with perfect holiness. When the God of Moses, Uzzah, and Isaiah touched down on the earth, Mary's womb was where he landed, and there was overcome the distance and alienation that had separated us from the Holy One.

We are now his friends. He walked among us and we touched him. His Holy Spirit indwells us. We eat his holy Food in the Eucharist. We no longer approach God with trepidation as though he is thundering from Mount Sinai; we boldly approach the throne of grace with "the spirits of just men made perfect" (see Heb 12:18-24; 4:16).

As one who has received redemption in its fullness, Mary models the grace available to all of us. Mary does not differ from us because she possessed these gifts of grace. We also possess them. She simply had them from the beginning of her conception, while we receive them in baptism and justification. Christ offers to all of us the same holiness, purity, and liberation from sin that Mary enjoyed.

If Mary remained a virgin, then who are the people that the Scripture calls the "brothers" and "sisters" of the Lord?

The Church has always accepted and taught that Mary remained a virgin throughout her entire life. As Pope Martin I proclaimed at the Lateran Council in 649: "She conceived without seed, of the Holy Spirit ... and without injury brought him forth ... and after his birth preserved her virginity inviolate." All but one of the Church Fathers; all the ancient Catholic and Orthodox creeds; and even the chief Protestant reformers, Luther, Zwingli, and Calvin, taught that she remained a virgin and was properly called "Ever-Virgin."

Throughout Christian history she is "the Virgin Mary," not "the once-and-former virgin, Mary." As Scott Hahn has put it: "Indeed,

Mary's identity is incomplete without the word 'virgin.'... Virginity is not merely a characteristic of her personality, or a description of her biological state. Virginity is so much a part of her that it has become like a name. When literature or songs refer to 'the Virgin' or 'the Blessed Virgin,' it can mean only one person: Mary."[10]

Occasionally, a heretic in the early Church would argue that Mary could not have been a perpetual virgin since the New Testament refers to the "brothers and sisters of the Lord."[11] If these passages were the only relevant texts, then we could probably retire the question by conceding that Jesus had blood siblings. But there are many other important passages, and even the above texts aren't as straightforward as they appear on first reading.

Since in Hebrew there is no specific word for "cousin," the word for "brother" is quite elastic and commonly refers to cousins or other kinsmen. The same Greek word used in these passages for "brother" is used in the Greek translation of the Hebrew Bible to refer to relatives other than blood brothers (see Gn 14:16; 29:15; Lv 10:4; 1 Chr 23:22). To complicate matters further, some of these "brothers of the Lord" are named, and we find them to be the sons of another Mary (see Mt 13:55; 27:56; Mk 6:3; 15:40). These latter references in Scripture suggest that these "brothers" were indeed relatives of Jesus other than siblings.

Sometimes people think that since Jesus is called Mary's "firstborn," a "second-born" or "third-born" necessarily followed (see Lk 2:7). This is a false assumption. "Firstborn" in biblical culture was a legal term that referred to the child who first "opened the womb" and who then had the preeminent right of inheritance.

"Firstborn" thus referred to legal status, not numerical placement in a list. In fact, in some cases, a second-born became the firstborn because the original firstborn had lost the right of inheritance. Being called "firstborn" implied nothing about future offspring. Indeed, one ancient Greek tomb inscription for a mother who died during childbirth read: "In the pain of delivering my firstborn child destiny ended my life." I think it fair to assume in this case that there was no "second-born."

Some argue that Matthew believed that Mary and Joseph inevitably had sexual relations after the birth of Jesus (see Mt 1:18, 25). But there is nothing in the original language of these passages that forces us to believe that what hadn't happened up to the point of Jesus' birth necessarily happened afterwards. In other words, Joseph and Mary's abstinence from sexual relations didn't require "correction" after the birth of Jesus.

Furthermore, if Matthew believed that Jesus had siblings, then how did the early Church, familiar with these texts, ever develop the notion of Mary's perpetual virginity? This tradition is difficult to explain if these references were ever understood to mean Joseph and Mary had normal nuptial relations. Also, if these passages are so clear, why didn't the chief Protestant reformers see them as a rejection of Mary's ongoing virginity?[12]

On the other hand, many passages and circumstances favor the perpetual virginity of Mary. For instance:

- No one is ever described as a son or daughter of Mary other than Jesus. This is fitting if he is the only Son of a widow, but odd if he is just one of many children. Why so many references to "brothers and sisters of the Lord" but none to the "children of Mary"? (Mk 6:3).

- If Mary and Joseph had other children, where are they in the story of Jesus' being found in the temple? It reads most naturally as though Jesus were an only child (Lk 2:41-52).

- If Mary had other biological offspring, why did Jesus, as he hung dying on the cross, violate Jewish custom and entrust his mother into the keeping of John, the Beloved Disciple? (see Jn 19:26-27). The next oldest sibling should have assumed responsibility for the mother.

- Moreover, belief in Mary's perpetual virginity appeared very early in the Church. Indeed, James, the "brother of the Lord," was bishop of Jerusalem and could have debunked the belief simply by stepping forward and announcing that he was a uterine child of Mary. Yet the early Church with almost no exceptions universally held to Mary's perpetual virginity. How did such a belief grow up while the memory of the "brothers and sisters" of Jesus was very much alive?

- To the angel Gabriel's announcement that Mary would conceive a son, she posed a strange question: "How can this be, since I have no relations with a man?" (see Lk 1:27-34, NAB). If Mary had planned on having normal marital relations with Joseph, the question would have been out of place. She would have enjoyed the marriage bed with her husband, and nature would have taken its course.

In all likelihood, she would have eventually conceived a son. Such a development certainly wouldn't have been unusual. But apparently that wasn't a part of her imagined future. Behind her question is the assumption that though she would soon be married, she wasn't planning on bearing children.

Whether she had vowed virginity from an early age or whether Joseph was marrying her more as a ward than a wife, we don't know. But she didn't expect to conceive a child and was surprised at the angel's announcement.

Mary's perpetual virginity cannot be understood apart from her being the Mother of God. Again, the Marian dogmas all begin with a reflection on the identity and significance of Jesus. To carry and give birth to the Son of God must have been the supreme fulfillment of her reproductive capacities.

Wasn't this the purpose for which she was "woman"? As someone has said, "We love all the babies of the world. We adore only one." Any future children would have been anticlimactic. Just think: If your first child is God, how do you think of number two?

Also consider what later siblings would have gone through. Younger children usually accuse the firstborn of acting like a deity: "Who do you think you are, God?" Well, yes, in this case, they would have been right. Imagine growing up with God as your older brother! I suppose you could argue that Jesus had to be an only child if only to spare later siblings serious self-concept problems.

So who were the "brothers of the Lord"? We don't know with a certainty. Like so many others on the pages of Scripture, their identity is not firmly established.

Throughout Christian history, the vast majority of believers have known they weren't the biological offspring of Mary. Apart from that conviction, however, the question is open. A few seem to be the sons of a different Mary not necessarily related to Mary, the mother of Jesus. St. Epiphanius believed they were the sons of Joseph by a former marriage. St. Jerome taught that they were the cousins of Jesus through a sister of Mary.

What is more important than resolving all the exegetical details, however, is to remember that we may be called to renounce some of the good things of this world for the sake of the gospel. At the annunciation, Mary said yes to a life of sacrificial love that cost her some of the natural goods of married life. No other woman had ever received the request to mother God in human flesh.

Nevertheless, like Mary, we too are birthing Christ into the world (see Gal 4:19) since Christ in us is "the hope of glory" (Col 1:27). Thus we offer him to the world by sharing the good news of the gospel, in acts of mercy and justice, and in renouncing our life in order that his life will abound and grow within us.

As St. Paul wrote: "[You are] my little children, for whom I am again in travail until Christ be formed in you!" (Gal 4:19; see also Rom 8:29; Eph 4:13-15; Col 1:27). Mary's perpetual virginity stands as a beacon of how intimately we can bear and know God when we are willing to say yes to whatever he asks.

Why do Catholics believe Mary didn't die?

We don't know whether or not Mary passed through death. Eastern Christians tend to say that she did. Western Christians tend to say she didn't. Both East and West teach, however, that she was taken bodily into heaven.

This event is called the Assumption of Mary and is not to be confused with the Ascension of Jesus. Unlike Jesus, who ascended to heaven by his own divine strength, Mary was lifted up by the muscle of Christ's resurrection power.

What is the basis for this dogma? Sacred Tradition calls Christ the Last Adam and identifies Mary as the New Eve.[13] The first Eve was to be the mother of all the living. Her rebellious partnership with Adam, however, led them to become the parents of death, not life.

In contrast, by obeying God, Mary conceived, bore, and parented the Last Adam, the Living One, Christ Jesus. In short, the first "Woman" bore sinners, the second "Woman" bore the Savior (see Gn 2:23; 3:20; Jn 2:4; 19:26; Rv 12:1-6).

Eve disobeyed the Word of God and delivered destruction upon us. Mary obeyed the Word of God and transmitted Life into the world. Had Eve made the choice of Mary, she would have never died. Mary, the New Eve who is supernaturally prepared to be the mother of the life-giving One, is not forced to pass through death.

The human race has begun anew in the Last Adam and the New Eve. Who would deny that Mary was as fully endowed as Eve? There is no great leap to infer that she, who was to cooperate in the redemption of the world, chooses with as much result and power as she who cooperated in the world's ruin.

The generosity of Christ's resurrection flowed first to the mother from whom he had literally drawn his physical body. Cosmas Vestitor, a Byzantine homilist of the mid-eighth century, noted that for Christ and Mary "there was the same burial and the same translation to immortality, since the flesh of the Mother and of the Son is one and the same flesh." Jesus doesn't sit enthroned in heaven, pointing at Mary and saying, "She used to be my mother." She remains his mother. The flesh he raised was her flesh.

The early homilies on the Assumption of Mary stress this ongoing palpable intimacy and indestructible bond between mother and Son.[14] Germanus, the seventh-century patriarch of Constantinople, imagines Jesus saying this to Mary at the time of her Assumption: "It is time to take you to be with me, you, my mother.... And so where I am, you shall be also, Mother, inseparable in her inseparable Son."

Love craves union with the beloved, and Mary was not to be left behind. "What son would not bring his mother to life," asked St. Francis de Sales, "and would not bring her into paradise after her death if he could?"

Even though Christians had been celebrating the Feast of the Assumption on August 15 since at least the sixth century, the Dogma of the Assumption wasn't formally defined until November 1, 1950, when Pope Pius XII wrote: "The Immaculate Mother of God, the ever-Virgin Mary, having completed the course of her earthly life, was assumed body and soul into heavenly glory."[15]

Although the Assumption of Mary is a singular privilege, Scripture does display many unusual departures from this world by those who walked especially closely with God. Consider that Enoch, Elijah, and those who came out of the tomb at Christ's death were all received bodily into heaven before the general resurrection (see Gn 5:24; Heb 11:5; 2 Kgs 2:1, 11; Mt 27:50-53). Further, those who are alive on earth at Christ's return will be "caught up" to him bodily (1 Thes 4:15-17).

Can we suppose that these believers should be so favored, but not God's own mother? As Newman put it: "Had she not a claim on the love of her Son to have what any others had? Was she not nearer to him than the greatest of the saints before her? And is it conceivable that the law of the grave should admit of relaxation in their case, and not in hers? Therefore, we confidently say that our Lord, having preserved her from sin and the consequences of sin by His Passion, lost no time in pouring out the full merits of that Passion upon her body as well as her soul."[16]

While the earliest documented stories of Mary's passing are severely tainted with legendary and extravagant details, they are too numerous to be written off as total fictions. They are too widespread to be simply the work of one group or to have originated in one particular theological setting. For all their shortcomings, they presuppose and bear witness to a historical reality that is further established by a telling omission: while two cities claim Mary's empty tomb, nobody claims her bones.

Very early on Christians venerated the saints and martyrs. Cities even competed to be recognized as their burial places. But surprisingly, no city ever claimed the bones of Mary. While claims abound for the relics of other old holies, we have no evidence that her bodily remains or cremains were ever venerated. Why? She had been translated to heaven. Nothing was left behind.

Whom did the seer of Revelation see in heaven at the end of the first century? "And a great portent appeared in heaven, a woman clothed with the sun, with the moon under her feet, and on her head a crown of twelve stars; she was with child and she cried out in her pangs of birth, in anguish for delivery.... She brought forth a male child, one who is to rule all the nations with a rod of iron, but her child was caught up to God and to his throne" (Rv 12:1-2, 5).

While the Apocalypse is highly symbolic and this maternal figure may personify Israel or the Church, yet it is inconceivable that first-century readers wouldn't also have recognized here Mary, the mother of the Messiah. This is why the Church has for centuries read this passage in the Mass on the Feast of the Assumption.

Christ loved his mother. He gave her a special share in his mysteries, as one would expect of a good Son. With her DNA, God prepared Christ's body in her womb.

How apt that she, who obediently donated her physical substance to the formation of Christ's body, should now be held up as a demonstration of the bodily glory awaiting all Christ's partners who lovingly bear him as the Word of redemption to the whole world. We will share his lot at the end of time, and fittingly, his mother has already anticipated our future glory.

Why pray to Mary and the other saints?

During the Easter Vigil liturgy the Church prays the Litany of the Saints, in which we ask the company of heaven to pray for us. The cantor intones, for example, "St. Augustine," and the congregation chants back, "Pray for us."

This litany swings back and forth for so long that we can imagine that "we are surrounded by so great a cloud of witnesses," and that we "have come to Mount Zion and to the city of the living God, the heavenly Jerusalem, and to innumerable angels in festal gathering, and to the assembly of the first-born who are enrolled in heaven, and to a judge who is God of all, and to the spirits of just men made perfect" (Heb 12:1, 22-23). The whole family of God in heaven and on earth is gathered for worship together.

Then the direction of the litany shifts as we address God and Christ. We no longer chant, "Pray for us," but rather, "Hear our prayer." Also, during the daily liturgy we request: "And we ask Blessed Mary, Ever-Virgin, all the angels and saints, and you, my brothers and sisters, to pray for me to the Lord, our God."

The difference is striking. We ask the saints in heaven and on earth to pray for us. We ask the Lord to hear our prayer.

Imprecision here generates needless controversy. Catholics are sometimes careless, and non-Catholics are sometimes suspicious. Misunderstandings abound because for many non-Catholics, prayer is the highest form of worship. For Catholics, on the other hand, sacrifice is the highest form of worship.

St. Epiphanius, for instance, condemned a fourth-century sect called the Collyridians who offered little sacrificial cakes to the Blessed Virgin Mary and then ate them. They were heretical, not for asking Mary to pray for them, but for sacrificing to her. Although all worship is prayer, not all prayer is worship. Prayers to the saints are no more a form of worship than asking the saints on earth to pray for us.

We appeal to Mary and the saints because some people have more intercessory clout than others. Jeremiah, long after the death of Moses and Samuel, heard the Lord say: "Though Moses and Samuel stood before me, yet my heart would not turn toward this people" (Jer 15:1; see also Ex 32:11-14, 30; Nm 14:13-23; Dt 9:18-20, 25-29; 1 Sm 7:5-9; 12:19-25; Ps 99:6-8). Judas Maccabeus saw a vision of two holy deceased men, the high priest Onias and the prophet Jeremiah, fervently praying "for the people and the holy city" (2 Mac 15:11-16). In the New Testament we find that those in heaven are offering up gold-en bowls of incense in which are the "prayers of the saints" on earth (Rv 5:8; 6:9; 8:3-4; see also Tob 12:12).

Throughout Scripture, believers are commanded to pray for one another (see Rom 15:30; Eph 6:18; Col 1:3; 4:3; 1 Thes 1:2; 5:23; Heb 13:18). Most of us pray for the friends who ask. Would our prayers for them cease if we were to die and go to heaven?

If "the prayer of a righteous man has great power in its effects" (Jas 5:16), how much more so the prayers of the one who is perfected in Christlikeness and standing before the throne of grace, face-to-face with God? The saints in heaven are mighty prayer warriors on our behalf.

Still the question: Why do we need to pray to Mary or the saints? Why not go to God directly? Didn't St. Paul write: "For ... there is one mediator between God and men, the man Christ Jesus" (1 Tm 2:5)?

Of course this is true. Sin has created a huge gulf between God and man. Man could not bridge that gulf. God himself took on human nature and crossed that divide.

St. Therese can't do that. St. Paul can't do that. But since Christ has done it, those who are united with him share in his work of mediation.

There is only one Shepherd, but there are many who shepherd Christ's flock (see Jn 10:14-16; Acts 20:28; 1 Pt 5:2). There is only one High Priest, but we all share in the universal priesthood of believers (see Heb 4:14-5:10; 6:20; 1 Pt 2:5-9). There is only one Judge, but at the end of time we will judge the fallen angels (see Jas 4:12; 2 Tm 4:1; 1 Cor 6:2-3; Rv 20:4).

In the same chapter in which St. Paul speaks of only "one media-tor," he also commands "that supplications, prayers, intercessions, and thanksgivings be made for all men, for kings and all who are in high positions, that we may lead a quiet and peaceable life, godly and respectful in every way. This is good and it is acceptable in the sight of God our Savior" (1 Tm 2:1-3). Even though Jesus is our Intercessor, we are commanded to participate in his intercession.

Imagine that the next time you ask a spiritual and prayerful family member to pray for you, he turns to you, stricken with horror, and rebukes you, saying, "Why ask me to pray for you? Go to God directly. I'm no mediator. Don't you know there is only one mediator between God and men, the man, Christ Jesus?" It's just not what you expect from a family member, is it?

Catholics don't believe in a "wall of separation" between heaven and earth. It's more of a permeable membrane. For the believing Christian, death is not some kind of meat cleaver that cuts off the relationship between Christians on the earth and those in heaven.

Christ is the vine; we are the branches (see Jn 15:1-8). Whether in heaven or on the earth, the believers remain the branches and are connected to one another through Christ, who is the vine. Death doesn't divide us (see Rom 8:35-39). We remain "one body" (1 Cor 12:20) alive in Christ Jesus, and thus we still support one another in prayer.

One of the great virtues of the Catholic and Eastern Orthodox traditions is that they keep alive our sense of the invisible universe. It's hard to believe in realities that aren't immediately present to us. Honoring the saints, asking them to pray with us, and celebrating their festivals help to remind us that we are not alone in this universe.

Catholics often give the wrong impression about the communion of saints. I'm reminded of a story about a little boy who wanted a bicycle. His parents didn't have much discretionary income, so they told him to pray: "You need to pray to Jesus about it, and maybe a bike will come."

He prayed but got no bike. So he asked his parents again. "Keep praying," they said. The pattern continued through Christmas, his birthday, and other holidays, but still no bike. Finally in desperation, the kid marched into his bedroom, grabbed the statue of Mary off the top of his dresser, wrapped it in a towel, stuffed it in the bottom drawer of his dresser, and said: "All right, Jesus, if you ever want to see your mother again, get me that bicycle!"

Mary doesn't engage in maternal blackmail. She's not the last resort if we don't get our way with God. It's wrong to imagine that Jesus is indifferent, and so maybe I can get his mother to answer me.

We solicit the prayers of those "friends of God" in heaven in the same spirit that we ask our brothers and sisters, "the friends of God" on the earth, to pray for us. God is the ultimate recipient of all prayer. St. Thomas Aquinas made an important distinction:

Prayer is offered to a person in two ways: first, to be fulfilled by him, and secondly, to be obtained through him. In the first way, we offer prayer to God alone, since all our prayers ought to be directed to the acquisition of grace and glory, which God alone gives, according to Psalm 84:11, "Grace and glory he bestows." But in the second way we pray to the saints [that is, ["holy ones"], whether angels or human, not that God may know our petitions through them, but that our prayers may be effective through their prayers and merits.

How can Mary and the other saints hear all those prayers?

Years ago someone calculated that Mary would have to "listen to 46,296 petitions at one and the same time, simultaneously, every second of time from one end of the year to the other." And that was just the rosary traffic. The one who calculated the number wanted to reduce to absurdity the ancient practice of invoking the saints. Only God could hear so much at once, he argued. Therefore, Catholics must really think Mary and the other saints are deities.

In response, we should note first that Mary and the other saints, of course, are not omniscient deities. Nevertheless, they do share something with God: they are outside of time. Being outside of time, it takes no time for them to hear these prayers.

Furthermore, there are a finite number of people on the earth, and thus a finite number of prayers are being sent skyward. Omniscience is not required—just an expanded range of human abilities. This is, of course, what God has promised: "What no eye has seen, nor ear heard, nor the heart of man conceived, what God has prepared for those who love him" (1 Cor 2:9). We also should think of the resurrected Christ's ability to appear where he willed without passing through doorways (John 20:19).

Second, we should note that our oneness in Christ forms the medium of our communication with those in heaven. He is the vine; we are the branches in heaven and on earth. We are one body animated by Christ, who is the infinite, personal God in heaven and on earth.

Since he wills the members of his body to communicate with one another, he guarantees the means by which they do so. The eye communicates properly with the brain, and the hand communicates adequately with the itchy nose. This is part of the "communion of saints," and it extends from heaven to earth (see Jn 15:1-8; 1 Cor 12:12-26).

Third, Scripture is clear that those in heaven are somehow aware of the needs of those on the earth. The angels in heaven rejoice over the repentance of one sinner (Lk 15:7-10); the elders and angels in heaven offer up the prayers of the saints on earth (Rv 5:8; 8:3); those under the altar know that the time of their vindication has not yet come on the earth (Rv 6:10).

While I'm not sure how the divine prayer switchboard works, I do know that those in heaven are united with us in Christ and are not subject to the same limitations of space and time that we are. They have a way of networking we know not of.

A Final Challenge

Ultimately, there is only one way of verifying the true nature of the Catholic faith and its understanding of revelation, Christ, sacrament, and Church. We must draw close to it to know it. Only as we journey along "the Way" of life (see Jn 14:6; Acts 19:23; 24:22) do we begin to develop eyes to see and ears to hear.

If we remain on the sidelines as spectators rather than participants, everything will remain spectral, abstract, merely a great idea or set of propositions. To shift metaphors, we must draw close to the fire to begin to feel its warmth.

Christ brings us the very life of God, not merely instructions about how to find God. Spiritually, we all need guidance and direction. We need maps. But maps are no substitutes for destinations. We want to experience Paris and London and Rome and not just listen to travelogues or look at a friend's slides.

As the Eastern Orthodox bishop Kallistos Ware has written: "Each is called to verify for himself what he has been taught, each is required to re-live the Tradition he has received. 'The Creed,' said Metropolitan Philaret of Moscow, 'does not belong to you unless you have lived it.' No one can be an armchair traveler on this all-important journey. No one can be a Christian at second hand. God has children, but he has no grandchildren."[1]

The Catholic Church is a divinely instituted mapmaker as well as the divine highway carrying us toward our destination of union with God. But the journey is yours.

Notes

Introduction

1. Caryll Houselander, *The Little Way of the Infant Jesus: How the Christ Child Leads You to God* (Manchester, N.H.: Sophia Institute Press, 1995), 96.

2. See, for example, Gn 1:4, 10, 12, 18, 21, 25, 31; Ps 8:4; Wis 11:17; Sir 16:24-30; Jer 10:12; 2 Mac 7:28; Acts 14:15; Col 1:16; Heb 1:2-3; Rv 4:11.

3. Consider the institutional implications of Acts 15; Mt 18:15-20; 1 Cor 5:1-13; 2 Cor 2:1-11; Rom 16:17; 1 Cor 1:10; 3:3-7; Eph 4:3-13; Phil 1:27; Ti 1:7-11; 2:15; 3:8-10.

I. Catholics' Relationship to Other Believers

1. Thomas Howard, *On Being Catholic* (San Francisco: Ignatius, 1997), 138.

2. *Unitatis Redintegratio (Decree on Ecumenism)*, 1; see 1 Cor 1:13.

3. Pope John Paul II, encyclical *Ut Unum Sint (That They May All Be One)*, 20:1; 49:2.

4. While the Church, through most of its history, has operated visibly as one, there has always been internal discord within the one Church (see, for example, Gal 1:6-9; 1 Jn 2:18-19; 1 Cor 1:11-13; 11:18-22). See also *Unitatis*, 3.

5. See *Unitatis*, 3.

6. *Unitatis*, 4; see also *Ut Unum Sint*, 1.2.

7. *Ut Unum Sint*, 1.2.

8. See *Unitatis*, 4.

9. *Unitatis*, 9-12.

10. See *Unitatis*, 3.

11. *Ut Unum Sint*, 99; see also 2.1; 23.1; 98.1.

12. *Epistle to the Smyrnaeans*, 8:1-2.

II. Scripture and Tradition

1. *Catechism of the Catholic Church*, 83; hereafter cited as "CCC."

2. On occasion the New Testament writers use the term in a negative way to refer to heretical traditions (see Col 2:8).

3. *Dei Verbum (Dogmatic Constitution on Divine Revelation)*, 10.2

4. *Dei Verbum*, 10.2

5. As Luther scholar Gerhard Ebeling has pointed out: "The manner in which Luther used this internal criticism of the canon is well known, though perhaps not as well known as it should be; he placed the Epistle to the Hebrews and the Epistle of James after the Johannine Epistles, and the unnumbered series, namely, the Epistle to the Hebrews, the Epistle of James, the Epistle of Jude, and the Revelation of St. John, outside the numbered sequence of the other twenty-three books of the New Testament; he also made value judgments, about 'which are the authentic and noblest books of the New Testament,' and corre-

spondingly negative utterances about other New Testament writings." Gerhard Ebeling, *The Word of God and Tradition*, S.H. Hooke, trans. (Philadelphia: Fortress, 1968), 120. The significance of this move may not be immediately apparent to many of us, but conservative Lutheran theologian John Warwick Montgomery acknowledges that Luther's bold rearranging of the New and Old Testaments was a way of marginalizing certain books as non-canonical. "His manner of cataloging them (Hebrews, James, Jude, and Revelation) apart as an unnumbered unit exactly parallels his way of dealing with the Old Testament Apocrypha." John Warwick Montgomery, ed., *God's Inerrant Word* (Minneapolis: Bethany, 1974), 81.

6. *The Works of Martin Luther*, vol. 6, C.M. Jacobs, trans. (Philadelphia: Muhlenberg, 1932), 363, 443-44.

7. In fairness to Luther, the early Church did have some disputes over the Epistle of James, but for reasons of suspected authorship rather than theological content. While Luther's appraisal of James improved over the years, "as late as the 1540s in his 'table talk' he was wishing that James be thrown out of discussion at the University of Wittenberg, for it did not amount to much." Raymond E. Brown, *An Introduction to the New Testament* (New York: Doubleday, 1997), 744.

8. The Greek and Russian Orthodox Bibles include a few more books than the Catholic, but that's another story.

9. See Mt 5:17; 7:12; 11:13; 22:40; Lk 16:16, 29-31; 24:44; Acts 13:15; 24:14; 28:23; Rom 3:21.

10. Compare, for example, Rom 1:18-31 with Wis 13:5-19; 1 Cor 15:29 with 2 Mc 12:44; Jas 1:19 with Sir 4:29; Heb 1:3 and Col 1:15 with Wis 7:26; Heb 11:35 with 2 Mc 7; 1 Pt 1:6 with Wis 3:5-7; Rv 1:4; 8:3-4 with Tb 12:15.

11. In fairness to Luther, he was aware of some of the debate in the

early Church surrounding the status of the Deuterocanonicals, including St. Jerome's early acceptance of the rabbinic canon rather than the Septuagint. Jerome, however, changed his mind and included the Deuterocanonicals in the Latin Vulgate. Luther was primarily driven by theological rather than historical/critical considerations.

12. G.K. Chesterton, *St. Thomas Aquinas,* in *The Collected Works of G.K. Chesterton,* vol. 2 (San Francisco: Ignatius, 1986), 427.

13. See First Vatican Council, *Dogmatic Constitution on the Catholic Faith,* c. 4 ("On Faith and Reason").

14. *Dei Verbum,* 8.

15. W.H. Lampe, ed., *The Cambridge History of the Bible,* vol. 2, *The West from the Fathers to the Reformation* (Cambridge: Cambridge University Press, 1969), 391.

16. *Dei Verbum,* 25; CCC, 133; quoting St. Jerome's *Commentary on Isaiah.* See also Pope Benedict XV's encyclical *Spiritus Paraclitus* and Pius XII's encyclical *Divino Afflante.*

17. *Dei Verbum,* 21.

18. Translators to the Readers: Preface to the Authorized King James Version of 1611, "The Translating of the Scriptures into the Vulgar Tongues," available in many editions.

III. Teaching Authority

1. 1 Clement 42:1-4; 44:1-3.

2. St. Ignatius of Antioch, *Epistle to the Smyrneans* 8:1-2.

3. St. Ignatius of Antioch, *Epistle to the Trallians* 3:1.

4. St. Irenaeus of Lyons, *Against Heresies* 3:3:1. "But where in practice was the apostolic testimony or tradition to be found?... The most obvious answer was that the apostles had committed it

orally to the Church, where it had been handed down from generation to generation. Irenaeus believed that this was the case, stating that the Church preserved the tradition inherited from the apostles and passed it on to her children. It was, he thought, a living tradition which was, in principle, independent of written documents; and he pointed to barbarian tribes which 'received this faith without letters.' Unlike the alleged secret tradition of the Gnostics, it was entirely public and open, having been entrusted by the apostles to their successors, and by these in turn to those who followed them, and was visible in the Church for all who cared to look for it." J.N.D. Kelly, *Early Christian Doctrines* (New York: Harper and Row, 1958), 37.

5. Walter A. Elwell, ed., *Evangelical Dictionary of Theology* (Grand Rapids, Mich.: Baker, 1984), 845.

6. See also Jn 13:1-11; Jn 18:10-11, 15-27; Mk 8:33; Mt 26: 58-75; Mk 16:1-8; Lk 22:54-62; Gal 2:11-14.

7. Alan Schreck, *Catholic and Christian: An Explanation of Some Commonly Misunderstood Catholic Beliefs* (Ann Arbor, Mich.: Servant, 1984), 83-84.

8. Raymond E. Brown, Karl Donfried, and John Reumann, eds., *Peter in the New Testament* (Minneapolis: Augsburg, 1973), 92; Gerhard Maier, "The Church in the Gospel of Matthew," in D.A. Carson, ed., *Biblical Interpretation and Church Text and Context* (Flemington Markets, New South Wales: Paternoster Press, 1984), 58.

9. See 1 Cor 1:12; 3:22; 9:5; 15:5; Gal 1:18; 2:9, 11, 14.

10. See, for example, J. Jeremias in *Theological Dictionary of the New Testament,* Gerhard Kittel, ed., Geoffrey Bromiley, trans. (Grand Rapids, Mich.: Eerdmans, 1968), 3:749-750; Raymond E. Brown, Joseph A. Fitzmyer, and Roland E. Murphy, eds., *Jerome Biblical Commentary* (Englewood Cliffs,

N.J.: Prentice Hall, 1968), 276; David Stern, *Jewish New Testament Commentary* (Clarksville, Md.: Jewish New Testament Publications, 1992), 54; W.F. Albright and C.S. Mann, eds., *The Anchor Bible: Matthew* (Garden City, N.Y.: Doubleday, 1971), 196; R.T. France, *Matthew: Evangelist and Teacher* (Grand Rapids, Mich.: Zondervan, 1989), 247.; Stephen Ray, *Upon This Rock* (San Francisco: Ignatius, 1999), 263-297

11. Isidore Singer and Cyrus Adler, eds., *The Jewish Encyclopedia,* vol. 3 (New York: Funk & Wagnalls, 1903-12, new ed., 1925), 215.

12. *Lumen Gentium (Dogmatic Constitution on the Church),* 25. See also Vatican Council I, Dogmatic Constitution *Pastor Aeternus.*

13. *Unitatis,* 7.

14. *Dei Verbum,* 26.

15. The decrees and declarations of the Council are to be read in light of the constitutions. The constitutions go to the heart of the Church, its "constitution." The decrees and declarations pertain more to pastoral and practical matters. While all the teaching of an ecumenical council is binding, the four constitutions of Vatican II provide an interpretive key for the other decrees and declarations. These are the documents of Vatican II:
   • *Dogmatic Constitution on the Church (Lumen Gentium)*
   • *Dogmatic Constitution on Divine Revelation (Dei Verbum)*
   • *Constitution on the Sacred Liturgy (Sacrosanctum Concilium)*
   • *Pastoral Constitution on the Church in the Modern World (Gaudium et Spes)*
   • *Decree on the Instruments of Social Communication (Inter Mirifica); Decree on Ecumenism (Unitatis Redintegratio)*
   • *Decree on Eastern Catholic Churches (Orientalium Ecclesiarum)*
   • *Decree on the Bishops' Pastoral Office in the Church (Christus Dominus)*

- *Decree on Priestly Formation (Optatam Totius);*
- *Decree on the Appropriate Renewal of the Religious Life (Perfectae Caritatis)*
- *Decree on the Apostolate of the Laity (Apostolicam Actuositatem)*
- *Decree on the Ministry and Life of Priests (Presbyterorum Ordinis)*
- *Decree on the Church's Missionary Activity (Ad Gentes Divinitus)*
- *Declaration on Christian Education (Gravissimum Educationis)*
- *Declaration on the Relationship of the Church to Non-Christian Religions (Nostra Aetate)*
- *Declaration on Religious Freedom (Dignitatis Humanae)*

16. John Paul II, Apostolic Constitution *Fidei Depositum (Deposit of Faith), On the Publication of the* Catechism of the Catholic Church, 3.

IV. Salvation

1. 1 Cor 6:10; see also Mt 25:34; Mk 10:17; Lk 10:25; 18:18; Eph 1:14; 5:5; Col 1:12; 3:24; Heb 9:15; 1 Pt 1:4; Rv 21:7. "[W]e are said to be justified gratuitously because nothing that precedes justification, neither faith nor works, merits the grace of justification" (see Rom 11:6; Council of Trent, Sixth Session, "Decree on Justification," 1547, as quoted in *The Christian Faith in the Doctrinal Documents of the Catholic Church,* J. Dupuis, ed. (New York: Alba, 1998), 747.

2. Mt 25:21; see also Acts 20:24; 1 Cor 9:24; Gal 2:2; 5:7; 2 Tm 4:7; Heb 12:1.

3. The Anglican historian of the doctrine of justification, Alister McGrath, acknowledges the novelty of the Reformers' views on justification: "A fundamental discontinuity was introduced into the western theological tradition where none had ever existed,

or ever been contemplated, before. The Reformation under-standing of the nature of justification—as opposed to its mode—must therefore be regarded as a genuine theological novum." Alister E. McGrath, *Iustitia Dei: A History of the Christian Doctrine of Justification*, vol. I (Cambridge: Cambridge University Press, 1986), 186, 187. Also M.J. Edwards comments: "Martin Luther could not have found his own account of Paul precisely stated in any of the Fathers, though he might have felt that Marius Victorinus and Augustine had a sound view of the primacy of grace in our elec-tion and our consequent good works." Mark J. Edwards, ed., *Ancient Christian Commentary on Scripture*, Vol. VIII, *Galatians, Ephesians, Philippians* (Downers Grove, Ill.: InterVarsity Press, 1999), xix.

4.   See also Mt 16:26-27; 25:31-46; Jn 5:24-29; Rom 2:5-8; 2 Cor 5:10.

5.   The logic behind this position runs like this: Christ's work on the cross is finished and sufficient to cover all your sins—past, present, and future. The moment you make a decision to trust in Christ for salvation, that moment is perpetuated for all eter-nity, and nothing or nobody, including yourself, can undermine your heavenly destiny. Frank Sheed, the noted Catholic preacher, tells of meeting a man in Hyde Park, London, who boasted: "I couldn't go to hell if I tried." This is an extreme case, of course, but this attitude does show up even in preaching sometimes. R.B. Thieme, founding pastor of Berachah Church in Houston, wrote: "You can even become an atheist; but if you once accept Christ as saviour, you cannot lose your salvation, even though you deny God." R.B. Thieme, *Apes and Peacocks or the Pursuit of Happiness* (Houston: Thieme, 1973), 23.

6.   See Mt 23:23, 12:5, 7, 12; 22:38-39; 5:19; 10:37; 5:22; 11:24;

12:32; Mk 2:27; 1 Cor 3:12-13; 11:30; 13:13; Lk 19:17, 19; Jn 15:13; 19:11; 2 Cor 5:10; 1 Tm 1:15; 1 Jn 5:16-17.

7. See also John Paul II, *Reconciliatio et paenitentia (On Reconciliation and Penance)*, 17.12.

8. See, for example, Mt 15:17-20; Eph 5:5; Gal 5:19-21; Rom 1:29-32. Many use the Ten Commandments as a test for mortal sin.

9. Sin bears both eternal and temporal consequences. Mortal sin severs our relationship with the eternal God. The consequence of such sin is eternal separation from him—hell. Faith in Christ, confession, repentance, and their fruits can restore the relationship (see Acts 2:38; Rom 10:9; 1 Jn 1:9; Jas 2:14-26). But there are also temporal consequences of sin that forgiveness doesn't blot out. Moses, for instance, is kept from entering the Promised Land because of his disobedience in spite of his repentance (see Nm 21:7-9; 27:12-14). David and Bathsheba lose the son conceived in their adultery in spite of their repentance (2 Sm 12:13-25). Zacchaeus repays those he swindled four times what he owes them. He makes restitution in spite of being forgiven (see Lk 19:8-9). Even venial sin bends our will in the direction of evil. Prayer and good works begin to bend it back. In the great purgation, purgatory, we are purged of the temporal consequences of sin.

10. Throughout Scripture, the "Day of the Lord" is described as being like a refiner's fire. See Mal 3:3; 4:1; see also Is 1:25; 4:4; Dn 12:10; Zec 13:8-9; Zep 3:1-13; Jn 15:1-6; Heb 12:7-11; 1 Pt 1:7.

11. St. Augustine argued: "That some sinners are 'not forgiven either in this world or in the next' would not be truly said unless there were other [sinners] who, though not forgiven in this world, *are* forgiven in the world to come" (*City of God*, 21:24; emphasis added).

12. "In Lk 23:43 it (paradise) is no doubt dependent on contemporary Jewish conceptions, and refers to the at-present hidden and intermediate abode of the righteous." H. Bietenhard, C. Brown in *The New International Dictionary of New Testament Theology*, vol. II, Colin Brown, ed. (Grand Rapids, Mich.: Zondervan, 1976), 762. Two other passages referring to "paradise" may well refer to heaven (2 Cor 12:3; Rv 2:7). But Luke refers earlier to a pre-resurrection resting place for the righteous as "Abraham's bosom." This is where the righteous dead go to await future vindication. The Talmud mentions both "paradise" and "Abraham's bosom" as the home of the righteous, but they are not the same as heaven. They are a "holding tank" until the day of resurrection, which Christians believe Christ inaugurates in his own bodily resurrection.

13. Sometimes in Catholic literature you will see the use of "days" and so on. This convention originated in the Middle Ages to create correspondences with penances on earth in the interest of maintaining a linkage between life here and life after death.

14. John Paul II, "The Holy Spirit and Hope," *L'Osservatore Romano*, English language ed., July 8, 1991, as quoted in Ralph Martin, *Is Jesus Coming Soon?* (San Francisco: Ignatius, 1997), 105-6.

15. St. Catherine of Genoa, *Treatise on Purgatory*, published under the title *Fire of Love: Understanding Purgatory* (Manchester, N.H.: Sophia Institute Press, 1996), as quoted in Martin, *Is Jesus Coming Soon?* 106.

V. Worship, Sacraments, and Sacramentals

1. St. Augustine of Hippo, *Letter to Januarius*, as quoted in William A. Jurgens, ed., *The Faith of the Early Fathers*, vol. 3 (Collegeville, Minn.: Liturgical Press, 1979), 3.

2. St. John Chrysostom, *Homilies on the Treachery of Judas*, as quoted in Jurgens, *Faith*, vol. 2 (Collegeville, Minn.: Liturgical Press, 1979), 104.

3. St. Ambrose of Milan, *On the Mysteries*, H. De Romestin, trans. in Philip Schaff and Henry Wace, eds., *Nicene and Post-Nicene Fathers*, vol. X (Grand Rapids, Mich.: Eerdmans, 1989), 324.

4. *Smyrnaeans*, 7:1.

5. Mt 28:19; Rom 1:7; Ru 2:4; Jgs 6:12.

6. See Ps 51; 4:3; 6:3; Mk 10:47; Mt 20:30; Lk 17:13; Rv 22:14-15.

7. See Tb 8:4b; Gal 4:6-7; Jn 15:15; 2 Cor 5:18-21; Jn 3:16-17.

8. See Lk 2:8-14; Is 9:6; 52:7; Ez 36:23; Rom 2:24; Eph 3:21; Phil 2:9-11.

9. See 1 Chr 16:36; Neh 5:13; 2 Cor 1:20; Rv 7:12.

10. See Dt 8:3; 1 Sm 3:10; Ps 81:9-15; Is 6:9-10; 52:7; Ez 3:1; 37:4; Mt 13:11; 23:37; Lk 1:38; 4:21; Rom 10:17; 15:4; Heb 1:1-2; 4:12.

11. Fr. Peter Stravinskas, *The Bible and the Mass* (Ann Arbor, Mich.: Servant, 1989), 52.

12. See Dt 16:10; Mt 26:10-12; 1 Cor 4:7; 16:1-2; 2 Cor 8:1-15.

13. See Ex 12:18; 23:15; Lv 23:6; Jgs 9:13; Ps 51:18-19; 104:15; Eccl 3:13; Is 25:6; Am 9:13; Jl 2:24; Mal 1:11-14; Lk 22:17-20; 1 Cor 5:7.

14. See Ex 12:24; Jn 6:51; Mt 26:26-29; Mk 14:23-25; Lk 22:19-20; 1 Cor 11:25; Heb 7:26-27.

15. See Gn 3:22; Ex 24:9-11; Prv 9:5; Is 25:6; Rv 19:9.

16. See Mt 5:23-24; Jn 14:27; 17:11; Rom 16:16; 1 Cor 10:17;

16:20; 2 Cor 13:12; 1 Thes 5:26; 1 Pt 5:1.

17. See Mt 8:8; Lk 24:35; Jn 1:29, 36; Acts 2:42; Rv 19:9.

18. John Paul II, *On Reconciliation and Penance*, 1984; 31, 33; see also CCC, 441.

19. C.S. Lewis, *Mere Christianity* (New York: Simon and Schuster, 1996), 55.

20. Mt 16:19; see also Mt 18:18; 28:16-20.

21. See Jn 20:23; 2 Cor 5:18.

22. In the first decade of the second century, Ignatius of Antioch wrote: "Let that be considered a valid Eucharist which is celebrated by the bishop, or by one whom he appoints" (*Smyrnaeans*, 8).

23. "The term 'priest' is etymologically a contraction of 'presbyter.'" F. L. Cross and E.A. Livingstone, eds., *Oxford Dictionary of the Christian Church*, 2nd ed. (Oxford: Oxford University Press, 1974), 1123. Aidan Nichols also points out: "In point of etymological fact, the English word 'priest' comes from an Anglo-Saxon contraction of 'presbyter.' ... The earliest evidence for calling presbyters 'priests' comes from memorials to deceased presbyters of the Asia Minor churches around 360, but it spread with remarkable rapidity in both East and West.... This was, of course, a natural consequence of the presbyter becoming the normal celebrant of the Eucharist, itself the principal manifestation of the priestly office of the ordained ministry." Aidan Nichols, *Holy Order: Apostolic Priesthood from the New Testament to the Second Vatican Council* (Dublin: Veritas, 1990), 50.

24. John Henry Newman, while still an Anglican, preached on December 14, 1834, that of the gifts and offices belonging "to Our Lord as the Christ," none can be named "which he did not in its degree transfer to his apostles by the communications of that Spirit, through which he himself wrought, one of course

excepted, the one great work, which none else in the whole world could sustain, of being the atoning sacrifice for all mankind." John Henry Newman, "The Christian Ministry", in *Parochial and Plain Sermons* (London, 1880), 304, as quoted in Nichols, *Holy Order*, 5.

25. The earliest documented ordination prayer dates from the early third-century work *The Apostolic Tradition* by Hippolytus (170-236), section 3: "Grant it ... to this your servant whom you have chosen for the episcopate [bishopric], to shepherd your holy flock, to serve you as your high priest, blamelessly ministering night and day, ceaselessly to propitiate your countenance, offering to you the gifts of your holy Church. By the high priestly Spirit may he have authority to forgive sins according to your command, to ordain according to your bidding, to loose every bond, according to the authority which you gave to the apostles."

26. See Jn 20:21-23; Mt 10:2-8; Mk 3:14; 6:30; Lk 6:13; 9:10; 11:49; 17:5; 22:14; 24:10; Acts 1:2, 26; 4:33; 5:12, 29; 8:1, 14-18; 14:4, 14; Rom 1:1; 16:7; 1 Cor 4:9-13; 2 Cor 4:7-12; 11, 12; Gal 1:1, 19; 2:9; Eph 2:20; 4:11-16; 1 Thes 2:6; Rv 21:14.

27. See Lk 8:1-3; Acts 6:1-8; Rom 15:8; 16:1; 1 Cor 3:5; Eph 3:7; Phil 1:1; 1 Tm 3; 4:6.

28. *Lumen Gentium*, 34. See also Eph 4:11-13.

29. 1992 Apostolic Letter of Pope John Paul II, *Pastores Dabo Vobis (I Will Give You Shepherds)*, 29.

30. 1983 Code of Canon Law, 1247.

VI. Spirituality and Morality

1. See Lv 16:29; 23:32; Nm 29:7; Jer 36:6; 1 Sm 7:6; Zec 7:1-7; 8:19; Est 9:31-32; Ezr 8:21-23).

2. 1983 Code of Canon Law, 1249, 1251.

3. Kevin Orlin Johnson, *Why Do Catholics Do That?* (New York: Ballantine, 1994), 203.

4. 1983 Code of Canon Law, 1237:2.

5. CCC, 67.

6. CCC, 67.

7. See 1 Sm 28:7; Is 8:19; 2 Kgs 23:24; Mt 24:24; 2 Cor 11:14; Gal 1:8; 2 Thes 2:9; Rv 13:14; 16:14; 19:20.

8. See Dt 18:10; Jer 29:8.

9. CCC, 2116; see also 2115, 2117.

10. For more on responsible parenthood, see Vatican II, *Gaudium et spes* (*Pastoral Constitution on the Church in the Modern World*), 45-51.

11. See Gn 21:1-2; 22:17; 29:31–30:24; Nm 11:12; Dt 28:4, 11; Ru 4:13; 1 Sm 1:6, 19; 2:20-21; Ps 100:3; 139; Hos 9:11; Ez 16; Lk 1:24-25, 58; Heb 6:14.

VII. Angels, Mary, and Saints

1. CCC, 330; see also Pius XII, *Humani generis* (*On evolution*), 26; Lk 20:36; Dn 10:9-14.

2. The Catholic Church also teaches that there are fallen angels (demons) led by a personal devil, Lucifer. See CCC, 391, 392, 414, 2851.

3. CCC, 336.

4. CCC, 487, 964.

5. "A mother without a home in the Church, without dignity, without gifts, would have been, as far as the defense of the Incarnation goes, no mother at all.... If she is to witness and remind the world that God became man, she must be on a high

and eminent station for the purpose." John Henry Newman, *Discourses to Mixed Congregations 18,* as quoted in Hilda Graef, *Mary: A History of Doctrine and Devotion,* vol. II (Westminster, Md.: Christian Classics, 1985), 108.

6. *Lumen Gentium,* 66; see also Ex 20:3; Rom 1:21-25.

7. Thomas Howard, *Evangelical Is Not Enough* (Nashville, Tenn.: Thomas Nelson, 1984), 87.

8. Pope Pius IX, *Ineffabilis Deus (Apostolic Constitution on the Immaculate Conception),* December 8, 1854; see also CCC, 490-93.

9. Perhaps the greatest historian of doctrine in the twentieth century was the Lutheran, now Eastern Orthodox, scholar Jaroslav Pelikan, who has written: "In its fundamental motifs the development of the Christian picture of Mary and the eventual emergence of a Christian doctrine of Mary must be seen in the context of the development of devotion to Christ and, of course, of the development of the doctrine of Christ. For it mattered a great deal for Christology whether or not one had the right to call Mary Theotokos.... It was a way of speaking about Christ at least as much as a way of speaking about Mary." Jaroslav Pelikan, *The Christian Tradition: A History of the Development of Doctrine,* vol. 1, *The Emergence of the Catholic Tradition* (Chicago: University of Chicago Press, 1974), 241-42.

10. Scott Hahn, *Hail, Holy Queen: The Mother of God in the Word of God* (New York: Doubleday, 2001), 103.

11. Mt 12:46-50; 13:55; 27:56; Mk 3:21; 6:3; 15:40; Lk 8:19; Jn 7:5; Acts 1:14; 12:17; 15:13; 1 Cor 9:5; Gal 1:19.

12. David Wright recognizes "the long established universal belief in Mary's perpetual virginity, which was endorsed by all the Reformers virtually without qualification." David F. Wright, *Chosen by God: Mary in Evangelical Perspective* (London:

Chosen by God: Mary in Evangelical Perspective (London: Marshall Pickering, 1989), 123. Calvin, in commenting on Matthew 1:25, considers those who would challenge the teaching of Mary's perpetual virginity on the basis of that verse "contentious troublemakers ... [who] foolishly and falsely inferred from the words of the Evangelist, what happened after the birth of Christ." John Calvin, *Commentaries on a Harmony of the Gospels, Matthew, Mark, and Luke*, vol. 1, David W. and Thomas F. Torrance, eds., A.W. Morrison, trans. (Grand Rapids, Mich.: Eerdmans, 1980), 70.

13.   See CCC, 411, 489, 726, 2618, 2853 as well as John Henry Newman, *Mary, the Second Eve* (Rockford, Ill.: TAN, 1991).

14.   John Saward has pointed out in the homilies of John of Damascus (c. 675-c. 749) on the Assumption "that just as the title Theotokos, God-bearer, is primarily Christological in reference and protects right belief in the Incarnation, so the implications of the same title constitute the foundation of belief in the Assumption; the Assumption too has an essential Christological reference, teaches us something about the person of Christ." John Saward, "The Assumption," in Alberic Stacpoole, ed., *Mary's Place in Christian Dialogue* (Wilton, Conn.: Morehouse-Barlow, 1982), 111.

15.   Pope Pius XII, *Munificentissimus Dei (The Most Bountiful God)*; see also *Lumen Gentium*, 59; CCC, 966.

16.   John Henry Newman, *Meditations and Devotions* (Harrison, New York: Roman Catholic Books, n.d. [orig. 1893]), 141-42.

A Final Challenge

1.   Kallistos Ware, *The Orthodox Way* (Crestwood, N.Y.: St. Vladimir's Seminary Press, 1986), 8.

KRESTA
in the Afternoon

Contact Al Kresta

Monday through Friday, 3:00 P.M. to 6:00 P.M. Eastern time on his live call-in radio program at 877-KRESTA-5 (877-573-7825). You can also listen live to Al and our entire line-up of fantastic radio programming 24 hours a day, anywhere in the world, at http://www.avemariaradio.net

Check out the weekly newspaper, *Credo*, online at http://www.credopub.com.
Or delivered to your home: Call our subscription hotline at 734-930-5200.

Click the Kresta message boards and check out all that Catholic Talk at http://www.avemariaradio.net.

For more teaching materials from Al Kresta, check out our outstanding catalog of fine products including teaching tapes (or CDs), complete interviews from past programs, books and other printed material, columns, and other monthly and weekly specials at www.avemariaradio.net